Frederic William Maitland

Roman Canon Law in the Church of England

Six Essays

Frederic William Maitland

Roman Canon Law in the Church of England
Six Essays

ISBN/EAN: 9783744773218

Printed in Europe, USA, Canada, Australia, Japan

Cover: Foto ©Lupo / pixelio.de

More available books at **www.hansebooks.com**

ROMAN CANON LAW

IN THE

CHURCH OF ENGLAND

SIX ESSAYS

BY

FREDERIC WILLIAM MAITLAND

M.A., LL.D.

DOWNING PROFESSOR OF THE LAWS OF ENGLAND
IN THE UNIVERSITY OF CAMBRIDGE

METHUEN & CO.
36 ESSEX STREET, W.C.
LONDON
1898

PREFACE

WHEN, in co-operation with Sir Frederick Pollock, I was at work upon certain chapters in a History of English Law, and, in particular, a chapter on marriage, I found that, on pain of leaving the book shamefully incomplete, I was compelled to make an incursion into a region that was unfamiliar to me, namely, that of ecclesiastical jurisprudence. After some study, which must not be called prolonged or profound, but none the less was unprejudiced, I discovered that I was slowly coming to results which, though they have not wanted for advocates, have not been generally accepted in this country by those whose opinions are the weightiest, and have recently been rejected by the report of a Royal Commission signed by twenty-three illustrious names. To be brief, I found myself attributing to the Roman Canon Law an authority over the doings of the English Ecclesiastical Courts such as it is not commonly supposed to have wielded. In the first three of the following essays (the other three deal with some minor but cognate matters) I endeavoured to state the reasons that had convinced me. These essays were published in the *English Historical* and *Law Quarterly Reviews*.

and I thank Messrs. Longman and Sir F. Pollock for consenting to their collection and republication. Now that they are brought together and, as I hope, somewhat improved, they may perhaps do a little to promote the further exploration of a not uninteresting tract of English history, and in that case I shall not regret a trespass which I am not likely to repeat.

At a time when the perennial stream of Anglo-Roman controversy has burst its accustomed channels and invaded the daily papers, the assumption will be readily made that anyone who writes about those matters of which I have here written is an advocate of one of two churches, the English or the Roman. Therefore it may be expedient for me to say that I am a dissenter from both, and from other churches. Probably that fact will be, and I think that it ought to be, of no interest to the readers of this book; but I have reason to fear the repetition of a mistake.

F. W. M.

CAMBRIDGE, 1898.

CONTENTS

CHAP.		PAGE
I.	William Lyndwood	1
II.	Church, State, and Decretals	51
III.	William of Drogheda and the Universal Ordinary	100
IV.	Henry II. and the Criminous Clerks	132
V.	'Execrabilis' in the Common Pleas	148
VI.	The Deacon and the Jewess	158

CANON LAW IN ENGLAND

I. WILLIAM LYNDWOOD

DURING the later middle ages the laws and the courts of the church claimed as their own so large a part in human affairs that any one who is interested in the legal history of England, even though his main interest lies in matters that are and always were not 'spiritual' but 'temporal,' is compelled to make some inquiry about the rules that were enforced by the ecclesiastical tribunals in this country. He would like, for example, to know something of the law of marriage that prevailed in England; he would like to know whether a certain decretal was a part of that law. Now, having been led to make some inquiry of this kind, it is my misfortune to find that I am unable to accept what appears to be, not only the generally accepted theory, but also the theory of those who have the best right to speak. It is likely that they are in the right and I am in the wrong. Nevertheless, the cause of truth may be served by the statement of an unfashionable opinion.

The doctrine that is in possession of the field I take to be that which is set forth in the learned Report of the Ecclesiastical Courts Commission. After saying a few words about the composition of the Corpus Iuris

Canonici, the commissioners (among them were historians whose every word deserves attention) gave us the following sentence: 'But the canon law of Rome, although always regarded as of great authority in England, was not held to be binding on the courts.'[1] Now if by 'the courts' the commissioners meant (and no doubt they did mean) the ecclesiastical courts, and if they were speaking of the three centuries which immediately preceded the Reformation (and no doubt they did intend to include that age), then I cannot but think that their *dictum*, carefully worded though it be, is questionable, and should be questioned.

It may be admitted that the difference between 'great authority' and binding force is somewhat fine; still it seems to me that the words here chosen suggest, and were meant to suggest, analogies which are to my mind misleading. The English ecclesiastical courts are supposed to manifest for 'the canon law of Rome' the respect which nowadays an English court will pay to an American or an Irish decision, or perhaps that higher degree of respect which one English court of first instance will pay to the decision of another, or perhaps some yet higher degree. But, at any rate, we must speak of respect, not of obedience. 'The canon law of Rome' was not regarded as statute law by the English ecclesiastical courts; they did not conceive that it proceeded from a legislator whose commands they were bound to obey. Now to me it seems that this doctrine, however often it may have been repeated, is not yet beyond dispute, and that in all probability large portions (to say the least) of 'the canon law of Rome' were regarded by the courts Christian in this country as absolutely binding statute law.

The exact measure of authority that was attributed

[1] *Report of the Ecclesiastical Courts Commission*, 1883, vol. i. p. xviii.

to the Decretum Gratiani we need not discuss. To start with, it was mere private work, one among rival text-books, and to the last it never received any solemn sanction. Nevertheless it soon drove all competitors out of the field. It became the one and only book out of which students learnt the old law of the church, and to which practitioners turned if, as would happen from time to time, they were compelled to refer to the old law. But so copious was the flow of decretals that when, in 1234, Pope Gregory's book was published, Gratian's was already antiquated. It was already a book for the lecture-room rather than for the law court. Almost all the topics that it touched (except, indeed, some few which were being extruded from the legal sphere) were regulated by new law, and many of the texts collected by Gratian were too hortative, too lax and flabby to satisfy an age which was severing an ecclesiastical jurisprudence from mere 'moral theology.'[1]

So perhaps we may put the Decretum on one side. But if we turn to the three collections of decretals that were issued by Gregory IX., Boniface VIII., and John XXII., there can surely be no doubt as to the character that they were meant to bear by those who issued them, or as to the character that they bore in the eyes of those who commented upon them. Each of them was a statute book deriving its force from the pope who published it, and who, being pope, was competent to ordain binding statutes for the catholic church and every part thereof, at all events within those spacious limits that were set even to papal power by the *ius divinum et naturale*. Our question, then, is not how much of a vague traditional law was accepted by the English

---

[1] J. F. von Schulte, *Geschichte der Quellen und Literatur des canonischen Rechts*, ii. 456: 'Der legislatorische Inhalt des Dekrets war zum grossten Theile bereits antiquirt, als die Dekretalen Gregors IX. erschienen.'

church and her courts, but whether those courts conceived that they were bound by three papal statute books which indubitably endeavoured to enact *ius commune* for the whole church.

In passing, two or three words should be said of this term *ius commune*, which was always in the mouths of our English canonists and their foreign brethren. It is a term which may lead an Englishman astray. In the thirteenth century our temporal lawyers borrowed it from the canonists, and this at a time when the English realm had little enacted law. Thus the lawyers of Westminster began to contrast 'common law' not only with local customs, royal prerogatives, and chartered *privilegia* proceeding from the king, but also with statutes, for statutes were rarities; and so it came about in course of time that in the Englishman's ear one of the chief contrasts to 'common law' was 'statute law.' But this is an English peculiarity. If we take up a modern German law-book, one of the first lessons that we learn is that *gemeines Recht* is not equivalent to our *common law*. By *ius commune* the canonist meant the law that is common to the universal church, as opposed to the constitutions or special customs or privileges of any provincial church. He did not mean to exclude from his 'common law' all rules imposed by a legislator. Far from it. Before the middle of the thirteenth century the most practically important part of his 'common law' was statute law, law published by a legislator in a comprehensive statute book.

Now the principal witness whom we have to examine, if we would discover the theory of law which prevailed in our English ecclesiastical courts about a hundred years before the breach with Rome, is indubitably William Lyndwood. He finished his gloss on the provincial constitutions of the archbishops of

Canterbury in the year 1430.¹ When he was engaged on this task he was the archbishop's principal official: in other words, his position made him the first man in England whose opinion we should wish to have about any question touching the nature of the ecclesiastical law that was being administered in England. He held the great prize of his profession. He had also been the prolocutor of the clergy in the convocation of Canterbury.² Of his learning and ability it would be impudent for me to speak; but, even if some of his citations of old books were made at second hand, it is plain that he was learned.³ He commanded a large library and had read many modern books, the books of Italian and French canonists. He refers not only to most of the great doctors of the fourteenth century, but also to Petrus de Ancharano, Antonius de Butrio, and Dominicus de Sancto Geminiano, all of whom lived into the fifteenth, and to Johannes ab Imola, who was still living. Evidently he was on the outlook for the newest literature (provided that it was strictly orthodox), and his travels on the continent enabled him to collect it. Probably we ought to have other works of his besides the *Provinciale*, for he speaks as though some of his lectures upon the Decretum were in circulation.⁴ Now we may well be prepared to hear from

---

¹ References will be made to the Oxford edition of 1679, in which the *Provinciale* is followed by the *Legatine Constitutions* with John of Ayton's gloss.

² Lyndwood, p. 192, gl. ad v. *provinciam*; see also *Dict. Nat. Biog.*

³ Is it not a trait of a somewhat unusual erudition that for an historical purpose he has gone behind the Gregorian collection to the *Compilationes Prima et Tertia*? Lyndwood, p. 126: 'Quae decisio habetur in compilatione antiqua, quam vidi et perlegi in tertia compilatione.... Quae hodie non habetur in nova compilatione decretalium, sed bene habetur in antiqua, ut prima compilatione, ubi eam vidi.'

⁴ Lyndwood, p. 299: 'Hanc materiam tetigi in Lectura Decretorum 22 q. 1 in prin.' Bale ascribes to him a *Summa Caustrum* and a commentary on certain psalms.

competent critics that in one sense he was no fair representative of the English canonists, since he was pre-eminently learned and pre-eminently able. The mere fact that he wrote a book raises him above his fellows. But I should suppose that in the main we may trust him to say what they think, and at any rate he will state the law that he administers in the chief of all the English ecclesiastical courts. His frequent employment in the king's diplomatic service would be enough to show that he was no mere bookworm. The very early date at which his book was first printed and the subsequent editions of it are a testimony to the high repute in which it stood before the Reformation. Since then it has been often cited, often lauded, sometimes read; but I cannot think that it has yet done nearly all the work that it is capable of doing for the history of the English church during 'the conciliar period,' or that it will do that work until it falls into the hands of one who is deeply read in foreign law-books.

As a witness from an earlier time we have the glossator of the *Legatine Constitutions*, whom it is convenient to call John of Ayton.[1] The main facts that we know about him are that in the canon law he was a pupil of John Stratford, who became archbishop of Canterbury; that he wrote his gloss while Stratford was archbishop,—in other words, between 1333 and 1348,—and that he was then, and had been since 1329, a canon of Lincoln.[2] Some further information about himself he

---

[1] Dr. Stubbs has adopted this form of his name. In *Dict. Nat. Biog.* he appears under 'Acton.' In Hardy's *Le Neve*, ii. 144, 233, he is Eaton. In MS. Camb. Univ. Ii. 3, 14 and the printed copies of his book he is Athon. The papal chancery seems to have called him Iohannes Iohannis de Acton —that is, John Johns of Acton (*Calendar of Papal Letters*, ii. 290).

[2] Joh. de Athon, p. 129, gl. ad v. *quod habita possessione*: 'Solutio secundum venerabilem patrem dominum Iohannem de Stratford doctorem meum, nuper Wintoniensem episcopum, iam vero Cantuariensem, in sua

may have wrapped up in a **riddle.**[1] The printed copies of his work should be **used with** caution, **for they contain references to** books **that were not written until after his day,** and the only manuscript **of it that I have looked at suggests that considerable additions** were made to his glosses by a **second hand. But,** unless the interpolations **are** extremely **numerous, we** may here also **see how rapidly foreign books were** received in England. The famous Bolognese doctor **Johannes** Andreae did not die **until** 1348, but already we have **abundant references to some** of **his treatises.**[2] **I should suppose that John of Ayton was very much** Lyndwood's **inferior in all those** qualities **and acquirements that make a great lawyer. He is a little too human to be strictly scientific. His gloss often becomes a growl against the bad world in**

repetitione dictae Decretalis *commissa*, lib. 6 [c. 35 in Sexto, 1. 6].' A *repetitio* was an academic discourse which differed in some points from a *lectura*. I am inclined to suppose that Ayton's book was written during the early years of Stratford's archiepiscopate, for though he knows the older legislation about procurations he does not refer to the *Vas Electionis* of Benedict XII. (1336). He speaks (p. 79) of the decay of England's military power. He could hardly have spoken thus after the victory of Crécy. The pope provided him with his canonry in 1329 (*Calendar of Papal Letters*, ii. 290). Johnson, *Vade Mecum*, ed. 3, vol. i. p. 152, says that John died about 1351, and cites for this a register at Lincoln. I am indebted to the kindness of the Rev. Christopher Wordsworth for this reference to Johnson's book and for a few more facts concerning our glossator.

[1] At the end of his work (p. 155) he speaks of it thus: 'Hoc itaque praesens meum opusculum in significatione triplici istarum figurarum 9, 2, 9, 5, 4 laboriose descriptum.'

[2] Thus in the Oxford edition at p. 21: 'quam approbat Car. de Zabarellis in dicta Cle. 1, *de re eccl. non alic.*'; and at p. 51, 'per dominum Marianum Socinum.' Franciscus de Zabarellis, the famous Zabarella of the council of Constance, was born about 1335, and did not become a cardinal until the next century (Schulte, ii. 283). Marianus Socinus was born in 1401, and died in 1467 (Schulte, ii. 319). Neither of these passages could I find in the Cambridge MS. mentioned above. Both John of Ayton and Lyndwood frequently cite *Car. Card. Cardi.* as a commentator on the Sext. The cardinal in question seems to be Johannes Monachus (Jean le Moine), who became a cardinal in 1294 (Schulte, ii. 191). In later days Zabarella was *the* cardinal of the canonists.

which he lives, the greedy prelates, the hypocritical friars, the rapacious officials.¹

Of the cosmopolitan, the 'extra-national,' or 'super-national' tone of the work of these two English canonists I need hardly say a word, except to point out that it implies the existence of a circle of English readers who are always looking to the mainland for new commentaries on the Decretals, the Sext, and the Clementines, and who would be ashamed if they fell behind their foreign colleagues in the conventional art of citation. Every one, it is assumed, will understand a reference to *Inno.*, or *Hosti.*, or *Spec.*, or *Will.*, or *Io. An.*; there is but one man who can be called the archdeacon, but one who can be called the cardinal. On the other hand, the names of any English canonists are conspicuously absent. They are conspicuously absent also in the catalogues of medieval libraries that have descended to us. Lyndwood's contemporary, John Newton, treasurer of York, bequeathed many books of canon law to the cathedral. He had works of Johannes Andreae, Zenzelinus, William de Mont Lezun, John de Lignano, Henry de Bohic, besides some older books, such as the commentary of Innocent IV., the Speculum of William Durant, and the archdeacon's Rosary; but never a book proceeding from an English canonist does he mention.² Are we, then, to believe that our courts and practitioners have succeeded in importing all this foreign science, and yet have rejected one of the main axioms on which it rests: the axiom that the popes can legislate and have legislated on a magnificent scale?

I have been unable to find any passage in which either John of Ayton or Lyndwood denies, disputes, or

---

¹ John (p. 68) holds that the *officialis* derives his title *ab officio*, i.e. *neceo*; Lyndwood (p. 105) protests.

² *Testamenta Eboracensia*, i. 364, 369.

even debates the binding force of any decretal. Of course there are portions of the canon law which, as a matter of fact, are not being enforced in England, because the temporal power will not suffer their enforcement. But that is quite a different matter; I will return to it in another essay. Here we are speaking of the law which our courts Christian applied whenever the temporal power left them free to hear and decide a cause, and I have looked in vain for any suggestion that an English judge or advocate ever called in question the statutory power of a text that was contained in any of the three papal law-books. As to those decretals which in Lyndwood's day were, and have ever since been, 'extravagant,' it would be difficult to prove that all of them were known in England.[1] With the publication of the Clementines in 1317 the gilded age of papal legislation came to an end; the golden age was already in the past. For one thing, the papacy was in a bad way; for another, so much law had been made that there was little room for more, unless it were to be of a new kind such as no pope would bring himself to make. The extravagants that were issued were few; they dealt with few topics, and those topics were not such as would often give rise to litigation in the English courts.[2] The ninety-six years which immediately preceded the date of Lyndwood's book saw the issue of only five decretals which passed into the classical volume of 'Extravagantes,' published by Jean

---

[1] John of Ayton seems to have known the three most famous extravagants of John XXII, *viz. Execrabilis, Sedes apostolica,* and *Suscepti regiminis;* see Schulte, *op. cit.* ii. 52. He also had *Cum inter nonnullos* 1323, which dealt with the dispute about evangelical poverty.

[2] Schulte, *op. cit.* ii. 53. 'Das eigentliche Detail des Rechts war erschöpfend ausgebildet; die päpstliche Gesetzgebung seit Clemens V erstreckte sich, abgesehen von den Erlassen für spezielle Verhältnisse, nur auf wenige Punkte.'

Chappuis.[1] Lyndwood, therefore, has very little to do with 'extravagant' constitutions; but if there are any which touch the matters about which he writes, he cites them as law. For example, the amount of money that should be offered to a visitor by way of 'procuration' is fixed by the *Vas electionis* of Benedict XII.[2] This instance may serve to illustrate the difficulties besetting any theory which would ascribe 'great authority' but no binding power to papal ordinances. The *Vas electionis* is an imperative document; it enacts a tariff. The pope expressly legislates for England among other countries. He says that an English prelate on the occasion of a visitation is not to receive more than a certain sum of money. Such a statute you can obey, or you can ignore; no third course is open to you. If you deny that it binds you, then you allow it no 'great authority'; you allow it no authority whatever. For Lyndwood it is law.[3] He admits that in England a custom has grown up which fixes the amount that an archidiaconal visitor is to receive; but in all cases that are not within this custom the *Vas electionis* should prevail.[4]

Other examples might be found of extravagants that John of Ayton and Lyndwood treat as law; but, for the reason already given, our chief concern must be with

---

[1] Jean Chappuis, who gave the *Corpus Iuris* its final form by adding two books of extravagants to the old statutory books, took part also in the Parisian edition of Lyndwood's *Provinciale*.

[2] c. un. Extrav. Com. 3, 10.

[3] Lyndwood, p. 221, gl. ad v. *personaliter*: 'quantum habent recipere nomine procurationis in pecunia . . . hodie limitatum est per constitutionem Benedictinam, quae incipit *Vas electionis*.' *Ibid.* p. 223, gl. ad v. *pecunia*: 'Haec tamen quantitas taxata est hodie secundum diversitatem certarum provinciarum, sicut patet in dicta constitutione Benedicti quae incipit *Vas electionis*.'

[4] *Ibid.* p. 224, gl. ad v. *solet solvi*: 'In Anglia communis usus habet ut nomine procurationis archidiaconus recipiat in pecunia . . . Ubi vero consuetudo summam procurationis non limitat recurrendum est ad ea quae habentur in Extrav. Benedicti quae incipit *Vas electionis*.'

the three officially published law-books. Now, if we regard the Gregorian code as a specimen of the legislator's art, it will seem to our eyes a very poor affair. The popes had gradually been converting a power of declaring law into a power of making law; they had declared law or made law chiefly by rescripts dealing with specific cases. When these rescripts, or rather the legal *dicta* contained in these rescripts, were collected by Gregory IX., the result was an inartistic and inorganic law-book. We might compare it to a rude compilation of 'head notes' taken from our reports, and solemnly sanctioned by the legislature. Again, we must remember that even the Sext and the Clementines, which are not open to exactly the same criticism, were in Lyndwood's day old books. Therefore there was ample need for gloss and comment, ample room for controversy. All this we may see in Lyndwood's work. There are plenty of open questions, plenty of cases in which the various doctors entertain various opinions about the meaning that should be found for this or that ambiguous phrase. Sometimes when they explain a text they will perhaps explain it away. But what we do not see in our English book is the slightest tendency to doubt the pope's legislative power, or to debate the validity of his decretals.

That in theory the sphere of papal legislation was circumscribed by the *ius divinum et naturale* was hardly to be denied. The pope cannot, says John of Ayton, change the foundations which support the church militant, such, for example, as the ten commandments and the seven sacraments, nor can he change the evangelical doctrine, nor can he deprive us of our natural right *vim vi repellere*.[1] But these limits are wide and elastic. Experience had been showing in decade after decade that the task of distinguishing between that portion of

---

[1] John de Athon, p. 76, gl. ad v. *summorum pontificum*.

the church's law which was to be called divine and that portion which had its origin in the decrees and customs of the church was of all tasks the most difficult. No one would say that every precept that could be found in the Bible was an irrepealable 'fundamental law' of the church. Many of these precepts were to be regarded as 'local and temporary' laws given to the Jews or the first Christians.[1] Finding no sure foothold in the Bible, the canonists had endeavoured to make a stand at the margin of the *ius naturale*. But this, again, was a line that could never be precisely defined. The play of thought round these matters is interesting to English lawyers, for we have a similar history to tell of our own modern ideas about the omnicompetence of English statutes. Coke would, if he could, have maintained some effective barriers against the advancing flood of acts of parliament. Long it remained a pious opinion that somewhere or other a limit there must be; but this limit was so far beyond the range of probabilities that no statute ever reached it. At length the very existence of any restraint was denied. But there is some difference between the two cases. We can afford to speak of unjust laws: of laws so unjust that it would be a man's duty to break them. The canonist could hardly do this; he could hardly admit that a rule could be both a wicked rule and the law of the holy catholic church. And so in speculative discussion the idea of a limit to papal law-making was preserved; but it was slowly receding into the region of the highly improbable and almost impossible. As a matter of fact, popes do not attempt to repeal the ten commandments.

[1] Lyndwood, p. 252, gl. ad v. *imagines*: 'Nec obstat Exodi 20, ubi dicitur *Non facies tibi imaginem nec sculptam similitudinem*, quia illud pro eo tempore erat prohibitum quo Deus humanam naturam non assumpserat. . . . Secus autem est postquam naturam assumpsit humanam.'

Having referred to this restriction, John of Ayton proceeds to discuss the question whether the pope is the *dominus* of all the churches in the world, so that he can take from one and give to another. The archdeacon (Guido de Baysio) in his *Rosarium* has, so John says, given a negative answer; but nowadays the other opinion prevails — namely, that the *dominium* of the churches belongs to the pope by way of reservation and collation; also the *dominium* of the goods of the churches belongs to the pope; for, whereas he is the governor of the whole, he can take from one and give to another, more especially if he has any reason for so doing.

And this power of the pope we daily feel to the uttermost in his frequent imposition of tenths. But, albeit the pope, while alive on earth, can, as I have said, turn things topsy-turvy, nevertheless, if he errs, his judgment will be the more terrible. Nor do I think that by such words as these I have broken the law against those who slander the pope, for in doubtful cases one is excused from guilt.[1]

John, then, can grumble about papal exactions, and, no doubt, there had been grumbling enough among the English clergy. But a moan, even when fortified by an allusion to the fate that awaits the wicked, is not a legal

---

[1] John de Athon, p. 76, gl. ad v. *summorum pontificum*: 'Contrarium tamen modernis temporibus tenetur, scilicet dominium ecclesiarum tam per reservationem quam per collationem ad papam pertinere, Extra. *de praeben.* c. 2 in prin. li. 6 (c. 2 in Sexto, 3. 4). Item et dominium rerum ecclesiae ad papam dicitur spectare: argumentum, 8 dist. *quo iure* (c. 1, Dist. 8), cum si[mi]libus no[tatis] per Willelmum de Monte Lauduno, Extra. *de praeben. si de beneficio* in Cle. (c. 5, Clem. 3. 2). Nam, cum sit gubernator totius universi, potest uni auferre et alteri dare, maxime ex causa: argumentum, C. *de fundis limitrophis. agros. li.* 11 (Cod. 11. 60. 3) cum si[mi]libus. Quam potestatem papae ad unguem experimur hodie in sua frequenti decimarum impositione. Sed tamen licet papa vivens in terris, ut praemissi, possit volvere quadrata rotundis, si tamen erret, iudicium sibi terribilius imminebit: ut legitur et notatur 40 dis. *si papa* (c. 6, Dist. 40) per Johannem Andreae et Hostiensem, Extra. *de conces. praeben. proposuit* (c. 4, X. 3. 8). . . . Nec credo quod per huiusmodi verba moderem in legem Extra. *de maledi.* c. prim. (c. 1, X. 5. 26), quia etiam in dubiis excusatur quis a delicto; argumentum, ff. *de iur. fisci, non puto* (Dig. 49. 14. 10).

principle, and we here see our English canonist citing a decretal which in the boldest language claims that a plenary power of disposing of every church belongs to the Roman pontiff.[1] If John thinks that he is at liberty to pick and choose among the decretals, his taste is strange. If there was a decretal that he might have rejected or passed by in silence, surely it was *Unam sanctam*, that stupendous edict in which Boniface VIII. asserted not only the spiritual but the temporal supremacy of the bishops of Rome. It had gone a little too far even for subsequent popes; it had been designedly omitted from the Clementines; and yet John must needs appeal to it.[2]

Lyndwood says that the pope may be tried by a council for heresy or for other crimes so gross that they savour of heresy.[3] He also allows that there may be cases in which a specific command given by the pope ought to be disobeyed: for example, a command that a boy should be provided with a benefice that involves a cure of souls.[4] All this, of course, is perfectly compatible with the pope's power of legislation. On the other hand, Lyndwood holds that no general council can be summoned without the authority of the apostolic see,[5] and he cites without disapproval the opinion of those doctors who maintain that the pope is above a general council.

[1] c. 2 in Sexto, 3. 4 [Clemens IV. 1265]: 'Licet ecclesiarum, personatuum, dignitatum, aliorumque beneficiorum ecclesiasticorum plenaria dispositio ad Romanum noscatur pontificem pertinere, ita quod non solum ipsa cum vacant potest de iure conferre, verum etiam ius in ipsis tribuere vacaturis.'

[2] Joh. de Athon, p. 122, gl. ad v. *a prelatis regni*: 'Nam et gladius terrenus gladio caelesti necessarie habet subici. . . . Patet in Extravag. Bonifac. 8, *unam sanctam*.' As to the omission of this bull from the Clementines, see Schulte, *op. cit.* ii. 48.

[3] Lyndwood, p. 95, gl. ad v. *se defendant*. Even the extreme curialists admitted the possibility of a trial for heresy.

[4] *Ibid.* p. 91, gl. ad v. *teneantur*.

[5] *Ibid.* p. 284, gl. ad v. *per ecclesiam*: also p. 16, gl. ad v. *authoritate concilii*.

It is the very eve of the Council of Basel, but not a word is said of what happened at Pisa and Constance, not a word of the schism, not a word of Pierre d'Ailly, or Gerson, or our own Robert Hallam. Not a hint is given us that Archbishop Chichele himself, to whom the book is dedicated, has lately incurred the displeasure of Pope Martin. The allusions to current affairs are of quite another kind. Cardinal Beaufort, at the pope's command, is leading a crusade against the Lollards of Bohemia, and by order of the apostolic see the bones of the heresiarch have lately been disinterred at Lutterworth.[1] Now, Lyndwood was making a text-book for beginners. Those to whom he addressed his work were *simpliciter literati et pauca intelligentes*.[2] He was not bound to call their attention to the seamy side of ecclesiastical polity, to speculate in their hearing about a possible conflict between popes and general councils, or to expose to their view the discomfort of the archbishop. Still, if we believe that there lived among the English canonists some treasured tradition of Anglican independence, we must admit that an unexampled and irrecoverable opportunity was lost when, in the days between Constance and Basel, the head of the profession wrote a book that was destined to be classical, and hurried past the momentous controversy of the age with a hint, or more than a hint, that the papal was the better opinion. Very recently the archbishop had plucked up courage and had appealed from the pope to a general council. And yet here to all appearance is his learned adviser telling him that any such appeal is vain *quia papa est supra concilium generale*.[3]

---

[1] Lyndwood, p. 284, gl. ad v. *Iohannem Wickliff*; p. 300, gl. ad v. *remotas*

[2] *Ibid.* p. 95, gl. ad v. *commenta*.

[3] Lyndwood, p. 104, gl. ad v. *fratrum nostrorum consilio*. The archbishop he says should not deal with arduous matters without the counsel

It would seem, therefore, that if we call Lyndwood a papalist, we are using that term in a correctly narrow sense. The question of the hour, the question on which the whole subsequent history of the catholic church must depend, is the question between pope and council, and Lyndwood lets us see that, in his opinion, the law is on the pope's side. This being so, we should be allowing ourselves an ample margin if we inferred that he was prepared to treat the decretals as statute law. It was very possible for men to contend that, though the pope had legislative power, an ecumenical council had a superior legislative power, could repeal papal statutes and establish boundaries which such statutes should not transgress. But we are not driven to inferences about this matter. Whatever may be the power of councils, the pope is the *princeps* of the church. *Quod principi placuit legis habet vigorem.*[1] The pope is above the

of his brethren. So also the pope, who, though he is *solutus legibus*, yet ought to conform himself to the laws. This is the opinion of Cardinalis (*i.e.* the French cardinal Jean le Moine, who died in 1313). 'In hoc tamen contradicunt alii doctores dicentes quod papa potest talia expedire sine eis, quia etiam ipse est supra concilium generale : *de elect. significasti, de concess. praebend. proposuit* (c. 4, X. 1. 6 ; c. 4, X. 3. 8). Et hanc partem tenet Hug(uccio) : 4 di. *leges* (dict. post c. 3, Di. 4), dicens quod ipse habet plenitudinem potestatis : 9. q. 3 *conquestus* (c. 8, C. 9. q. 3) : et idem dicit de imperatore, ut scilicet possit quaecumque ad eum spectantia sine consilio baronum suorum facere. Nec est credendum Iohanni Monacho qui erat cardinalis et suspectus erat quod voluit sustinere causam propriam, sicut ista notat Dominicus de Sancto Geminiano.' The passage here printed within inverted commas is taken with little change from Geminiano's commentary on the Sext, where, however, the important word *generale* does not occur. At least it does not occur in the Lyons edition of 1520 ; see f. 245 dors. Whatever Lyndwood's private opinion may have been (and with that we are not concerned), his public teaching seems to go the full length of setting the pope above a general council. The opposite opinion is represented as being held only by one doctor, who has been dead for upwards of a century, and who is suspected of self-interest. And this after the Council of Constance !

[1] Lyndwood, p. 28, gl. ad v. *expresse* : 'Et hoc verum puto in alio quam in papa. Secus tamen dicerem in papa : et est ratio, quia papa est supra iura, C. *de legi.* l. *digna* d. 1. 14. 4, ff. *de legibus*, l. *princeps* [Dig. 1.

law.¹ Any general constitution made by the pope is binding two months after its publication, even on those who are ignorant of it.² The decretals **stand on a level** with the canons of councils.³ To dispute **the** authority of a decretal is to be guilty of heresy **at a time when** obstinate heresy is a capital crime.⁴

This last is no private opinion of a glossator; **it is a** principle to which the archbishop, bishops, and clergy of the province of Canterbury have adhered by solemn words. Anyone who calls in question the authority of a decretum, **of a decretal, or** of a **provincial or** synodal constitution, **is a heretic, and, unless he will recant and abjure**, must **be burnt alive.**⁵ No doubt this enormous

---

3. 31]. Et in eo sufficit pro ratione voluntas, Inst. *de iure natu.* § *sed et quod principi* Inst. 1, 2, § 6]).'

¹ Lyndwood, p. 321, gl. ad v. *interdicto* : 'Et hoc verum praeterquam in papa qui non subiacet legibus, ff. *de legi.* l. *princeps* [Dig. 1. 3. 31].'

² *Ibid.* p. 51, gl. ad v. *excommunicationum sententiae* : 'Constitutio vero papae generalis post duos menses computandos a tempore publicationis eiusdem generaliter factae in consistorio ligat etiam ignorantes.' So also p. 19, gl. ad v. *publicam notionem*. The theory about the two months was derived from Nov. 66 (Hinschius, *Kirchenrecht*, iii. 777, note 1).

³ *Ibid.* p. 297, gl. ad v. *decretalibus* : 'Et nota quod decretales summorum pontificum sunt eiusdem auctoritatis sicut decreta quae sunt in corpore canonum digesta, 19 Dist. quasi per totum. Parificantur etiam canonibus conciliorum, 20 Dist. per totum.'

⁴ *Ibid.* p. 292, gl. ad v. *declarentur* : 'Dicitur etiam haereticus qui ex contemptu Romanae ecclesiae contemnit servare ea quae Romana ecclesia statuit, et etiam qui despicit et negligit servare decretales.' *Ibid.* p. 38, gl. ad v. *reluctantes* : 'Potest tamen esse quod aliquis violet canones credens quod ecclesia Romana non habet potestatem canones condendi; et talis punitur ut haereticus.'

⁵ Const. Tho. Arundel (Wilkins, *Concilia*, iii. 317) : 'Nullus quoque de articulis terminatis per ecclesiam, prout in decretis, decretalibus, constitutionibus nostris provincialibus, sive locorum synodalibus continetur, nisi ad habendum verum intellectum eorundem, et hoc expresso, publice vel occulte disputare praesumat, aut auctoritatem eorundem decretorum, decretalium aut constitutionum, potestatemve condentis eadem in dubium revocet, sive contra determinationem eorundem doceat, et praesertim circa adorationem crucis gloriosae. . . . Contrarium autem asserens, docens, praedicans, ac pertinaciter innuens, nisi resipiscat sub modo et forma praedictis, et abiuret, ut supradictum est, poenas haeresis et relapsi eventum incurrat.' Lynd-

declaration went beyond the practical intentions of those who uttered it. It was aimed at men who were rightly or wrongly supposed to be striking at fundamental articles of the catholic faith and worship. We must read it also as subject to explanation, for certainly we may and must dispute and deny the authority of a provincial constitution if it collides with a decretal; Lyndwood himself, as we shall soon see, is compelled to do this, or rather does it as a matter of course. But in the most general phrases and by the most terrible ban the sanctity of the decretals is to be upholden. Let us make no mistake about the meaning of this declaration. No conciliar action is necessary for the establishment of those decretals which are to be protected by the flames against all impugners. A decretum, says Lyndwood, is what the pope has ordained with the counsel of his cardinals when no one has consulted him; a decretal is what the pope either with or without the cardinals has ordained when anyone has consulted him.[1] There is to be no picking and choosing, no rejection even of the wilder 'extravagants'; the decretals are laws. But, further, they are, in Archbishop Arundel's phrase, *praecepta legum et canonum ab aeternae vitae et mortis clavigero, vicem non puri hominis sed veri Dei gerente in terris, et cui ipse Deus caelestis imperii iura commisit, rite edita, canonice promulgata.*[2]

But we must not catch at a few sentences, uttered,

wood (p. 298) understood this to extend far beyond matters of faith: 'Si non liceat disputare de his quae per ecclesiam statuta sunt quoad mores hominum, ut hic, multo magis non licebit disputare de articulis fidei vel sacramentis ecclesiae.'

[1] Lyndwood, p. 272, gl. ad v. *decreti*: 'Et dicitur decretum quod statuit papa de consilio cardinalium suorum ad nullius consultationem. . . . Canon dicitur id quod statuitur in universali concilio. . . . Decretalis epistola est quam statuit papa vel solus, vel cum cardinalibus ad consultationem alicuius.'

[2] Wilkins, *Concilia*, iii. 314.

perhaps, in a moment of terror, for in the presence of heresy the champions of the orthodox tradition will sometimes say more than they mean. Let us look at Lyndwood's method, the scheme and theory of his book.

Lyndwood has collected and digested the archiepiscopal constitutions of the southern province.[1] He provides them with a gloss. His position is that of a lawyer who is commenting on the edicts issued by a non-sovereign legislator. He has to consider whether and how they can be harmonised with a large body of law which that legislator has no power to repeal or to override. The archbishop may make for his province statutes which are merely declaratory of the *ius commune* of the church, statutes which recall it to memory, statutes which amplify it and give to it a sharper edge. He may supplement the papal legislation; but he has no power to derogate from, to say nothing of abrogating, the laws made by his superior.[2]

From this it follows that about any archiepiscopal

---

[1] He held himself free to reject not only obsolete constitutions, but also what he regarded as obsolete parts of effective constitutions. He modelled his procedure on that of St. Raymond. Perhaps he hoped that Chichele would follow the example of Gregory IX., and give statutory force to the constitutions in their digested form, though, of course, no statutory force would be given to the gloss.

[2] Lyndwood, p. 70, gl. ad v. *iuramento*: 'Possunt namque achiepiscopi et episcopi constitutiones facere iuris communis declaratorias et revocatorias, et ubi poena deficit in iure possunt poenas apponere et veterem poenam augere. Possunt etiam constitutionibus papalibus addere et eas supplere et ad correctionem morum statuta facere praeceptoria, prohibitoria et poenalia, dum tamen ius commune non subvertant, secundum Hostiensem, qui hoc notat in d. c. *ut singulae* (c. 4, X. 1. 24) et idem Jo[hannes] in notis post eum. Possunt etiam in his, quae ad ipsorum iurisdictionem pertinent, statuta facere, dum tamen legibus generalibus non obsistant prout notatur per Jo[hannem] An[dreae] in notis Extra *de off. le.* c. ultimo in principio (c. 16, X. 1. 30).' A constitution 'revocatory' of the common law is not a constitution that repeals the common law, but one which recalls and restores it. For this use of *revocare* see Lyndwood's Preface; he sets about his work because he thinks that the provincial constitutions are *pristino studio revocandae*.

constitution we may always raise the question whether it be not *ultra vires statuentis*. Lyndwood sitting as a judge in the provincial court would have held himself bound to allow that question to be raised. He himself has set the example by raising it on more than one occasion. Let us see how he treats it.

Against 'pluralities' there had been severe legislation. A decree of the fourth Lateran Council (1215) had declared that in certain cases if a man having one benefice obtained another, he was *ipso iure* deprived of the first.[1] In 1268 a constitution of the legate Ottobon decreed that the second institution of such a pluralist should be void *ipso iure*.[2] Then in 1279 Archbishop Peckham dealt with this matter. He remarked that the decree of the Lateran Council deprived the pluralist of the former of his two benefices, and that the legatine constitution deprived him of the latter, and then spoke thus: 'We, being unwilling to heap rigour on rigour, and considering the spirit of these two constitutions, neither of which deprives the pluralist of both benefices, and mixing mercy (*misericordiam*) with rigour, do permit (*permittimus*) that the pluralist may retain the latter benefice.'[3] Now this was not a very bold essay in legislation, and the archbishop expressly professed to be giving effect to the spirit of the existing law. Nevertheless, Lyndwood held that Peckham's constitution was

---

[1] c. 28, X. 3. 5.
[2] Const. Ottob. *Christianae* (Joh. de Athona, p. 126).
[3] Const. Jo. Peckham, *Audistis*: ... 'praecavere tamen volentes ne rigorem videamur coacervare rigori: mentem etiam constitutionum tam Concilii Generalis quam etiam Ottoboni clarius advertentes, quarum neutra et praeobtentis et ultimo simul privat. ... Nos tamen misericordiam cum rigore miscentes, non tam misericorditer quam prudenter permittimus, ut is qui plura beneficia curam animarum habentia absque dispensatione apostolica fuerit assecutus, ultimum beneficium sic obtentum retineat, et eodem iuxta tenorem Concilii Generalis de nostra speciali gratia sit contentus. ...' See also Wilkins, *Concilia*, ii. 34.

for the more part void. Here is his gloss on the word *misericordiam* :—

> Note that this mercy should rather be called injustice. For the mercy shown by the author of this decree is expressly contrary to a decree of the second Council of Lyons contained in the Sext, which neither the archbishop nor anyone lower than the pope can repeal or alter.[1]

Then to the word *permittimus* Lyndwood sets this gloss :—

> This permission can do nothing to prevent the law of the superior [*i.e.* the pope] from prevailing ; unless, perhaps, you say that it is valid so far as regards the person who gives the permission [*i.e.* the archbishop], so that he cannot impugn the second title of the pluralist ; for, as regards the person to whom the permission is given, we must receive rather what the law says about the matter than what is said by the person who gives, but has no power to give, the permission ; for such a permission, which is really no better than a mere tolerance, cannot excuse him who receives it from being bound by the law of the superior legislator.[2]

And then we learn that any constitution which Peckham may have made is overridden by later law : namely, by John XXII.'s *Execrabilis*, an 'extravagant' decretal which any champion of national churches would be glad to leave unnoticed, for it contains a startling

---

[1] Lyndwood, p. 136, gl. ad v. *Nos misericordiam* : 'Et nota quod ista misericordia potius dici potest iniustitia. Nam misericordia, quam hic ostendit huius decreti auctor, est expresse contra Decre. *Ordinarii locorum, de offi. ordi.* § ult. li. 6 [c. 3 in Sexto, t. 16, Gregorius X. in generali Concilio Lugdunensi], quam tollere vel alterare non potest archiepiscopus, nec aliquis papa inferior.'

[2] *Ibid.* p. 136, gl. ad v. *permittimus* : 'Ista permissio nihil potest operari, quin locum habeat lex superioris : nisi forsan dicas quod valeat quoad ipsum permittentem, ut scilicet ipse non possit titulum talis impugnare. Ex parte namque eius cui hoc permittitur potius debemus recipere quod in hoc casu a iure statuitur, quam quod ab ipso, qui circa hoc potestatem non habet, permittitur, iuxta notata per Cardi[n]alem, *de aeta. et quali. ordi. c. permittimus,* glo. 1. h. 6 [c. un. in Sexto, 1. 10]. Talis namque permissio, quae nihil aliud est quam quaedam tolerantia, ut notatur 3 di. *omnis autem lex* [c. 4, Dist. 3] per Io[hannem], non potest excusare eum cui fit talis permissio quin ligetur lege superioris aliud statuentis, ut praedixi.'

'reservation,' but which both Lyndwood and John of
Ayton cite as an unquestionable part of the law of the
church.¹ This *Execrabilis* was one of those greedy
extravagants against which in Lyndwood's time even
the moderate reformers were inveighing; there was no
chance of its being consistently enforced in England;
statutes of 'provisors' and 'praemunire' stood in the
way; still, until it should be repealed, it was an unquestionable part of the law of the church. And, by the
way, thanks to Mr. Bliss, we have lately acquired some
curious evidence of the clean sweep which this decretal
effected in England while it was a very new broom. It
was issued in November 1317;² in the summer of 1318
Pope John was giving himself the pleasure of filling up
some fifty English benefices that had been vacated by
the cession of pluralists.³

In the same constitution Peckham declares that
certain forms of pluralism are to involve the offender
ipso facto in a sentence of excommunication. Lyndwood
says that this declaration is new law; it goes beyond
the common law; therefore its validity must be discussed. The common law forbids a man to hold two
benefices by way of institution, or two by way of
commendation. Now the archbishop is within his rights
in affixing the penalty of excommunication to a breach
of this prohibition, for archbishops may add to the
constitutions of the Roman pontiffs, provided that the
substance is preserved.⁴ But Lyndwood suggests (very

---

¹ Lyndwood, p. 136, gl. ad v. *nec ultimo*: 'Hodie vero ista poena aucta
est per Extrav. *execrabilis*.' This decretal appears as c. un. Extrav. Ioh.
XXII. 3. John of Ayton often refers to it, *e.g.* pp. 23, 35, 46, 51, 85.

² Friedberg, *Corp. Iur. Can.* ii. col. 1209.

³ Bliss, *Calendar of Papal Letters*, ii. 171-182.

⁴ Lyndwood, p. 137, gl. ad v. *innodatus*: 'Quoad obtinentes simul sine
dispensatione plura beneficia incompatibilia bene potest stare haec poena,
de qua alias nihil statutum est, maxime cum archiepiscopi possint ad con-

unnecessarily, as it seems to me) that Peckham's constitution might be read as an endeavour to do more than this, and as an attempt to make illegal what according to the common law is sometimes legal— namely, the simultaneous tenure of one benefice by way of institution and another by way of commendation. Lyndwood thinks that Peckham's constitution does not make this futile attempt; but he says plainly that if the attempt is made it is futile. A decretal of Gregory IX. stands in the way. It is in some cases lawful for a man to hold two churches, the one *intitulatam*, the other *commendatam*.¹ If Peckham has threatened with excommunication a man who is doing what the general law permits, that threat is void. The constitution of an inferior, albeit a penalty is affixed, cannot repeal or restrict the law decreed by a superior. A right given by papal law must not be impugned even obliquely by provincial law.²

There had, again, been frequent legislation directed against the practice of letting churches and sources of ecclesiastical revenue to farm. In 1342 Archbishop Stratford, with the approbation of his provincial council, endeavoured to increase the efficiency of the law.³ Having referred to certain previous constitutions, he

stitutiones Romanorum pontificum addere, salva ipsarum substantia, ut notatur per Hostiensem et Iohannem Andreae.'

¹ Lyndwood, p. 137, gl. ad v. *aliud titulo commendae*: 'Contra istud opponitur *de elec*. c. *dudum* 2, § *partibus ergo*, ver. *insuper* [c. 54, X. 1. 6] et 21, q. 1, *qui plures* [c. 3, C. 21, q. 1], in quibus patet expresse quod licet unam ecclesiam habere intitulatam et aliam commendatam. Et sic sentiunt doctores communiter, d. c. *nemo deinceps*, ver. *unam*, li. 6 [c. 15 in Sexto, 1. 6], unde, secundum praemissa, hoc quod hic dicitur stare non potest, ut videtur.'

² *Ibid*. p. 137, gl. ad v. *immodatus*: 'Sed in obtinentes unam ecclesiam intitulatam, aliam commendatam, non posset habere locum haec poena, scilicet excommunicationis latae, nisi ut infra dicam, quia hoc esset restringere potestatem concessam a superiore, saltem per obliquum, quod non licet, *de reg. iu. cum quid* li. 6. . . . Non potest ergo constitutio etiam poenalis alicuius inferioris dictam legem superioris tollere vel refrenare.'

³ Const. Jo. Stratford, *Licet bonae* (Wilkins, *Concilia*, ii. 704).

says that the *religiosi*, the professed in religion, assert that those constitutions do not bind them. About this matter Lyndwood takes their side.[1] Then Stratford, with the sanction of the council, ordains that if the religious let their benefices or their portions of tithes to laymen, or (without the consent of the diocesan bishop) to clerks, they are to suffer a certain penalty. Lyndwood has the gravest doubts as to the validity of this legislation. When first he turns to the constitution, he observes that we do not know whether there were present at the council all those whose presence was necessary for the validity of this statute. 'This I say because several things that are here ordained seem to be repugnant to the common law.'[2] Later on he suggests an interpretation of the constitution which may make it harmless, but holds that, if this interpretation be rejected, and if the constitution tries to curtail the rights given to the religious by the *ius commune*, then it must depend for its validity on the consent, express or tacit, of the monks. As to the 'exempt' religious, they are not bound by this statute unless they expressly consented to it.[3] As to the others, they may perhaps be bound if they were present and raised no objection; but this is a doubtful point, for what we read in Johannes Andreae would seem to demand an express consent. In short, we may save this statute if we can prove that the religious consented, or if (and this is what Lyndwood would do) we say that it did not seriously affect them; but nothing is clearer than that an English pro-

---

[1] Lyndwood, p. 157, gl. ad v. *asserunt non ligare*: 'Et bene ut videtur.'
[2] *Ibid.* p. 154, gl. ad v. *provinciali concilio*: 'Quae personae interfuerunt in hoc concilio, an videlicet omnes quarum interfuit quoad validationem huius statuti, ignoratur. Haec dico propter ea quae hic statuuntur, et ut melius advertas quae infra dicam: nam plura hic ordinata videntur iuri communi repugnantia.'
[3] *Ibid.* p. 160, gl. ad v. *de cetero*.

vincial council has no power to restrict a right conferred by a decretal of Innocent III. which is contained in the Gregorian statute-book.[1]

Nor is it merely by papal decretals that the legislative powers of the archbishop are curtailed. The pope, of course, is his superior, but so is a legate sent here *a latere*. No English prelate, no English council, has any power to repeal or override the statutes set by Otto and Ottobon.[2] Nay, more: no English prelate, no English council, has any power to put a statutory interpretation upon those statutes. Archbishop Peckham in his provincial council may have incautiously used words which might seem to claim such a power. Lyndwood meets the possible objector: True it is that, if there is any real room for doubt about the meaning of the statute, then the statute-maker, and none other, can interpret it. But in the case before us the words of the legate Ottobon are unambiguous and plain enough; so it is lawful for an 'inferior prelate' (*e.g.* the archbishop in his provincial council) to declare their meaning.[3] In other words, our doctrine is that the archbishop can set an interpretation on a legatine constitution, provided

---

[1] Lyndwood, p. 160, gl. ad v. *laicis quovismodo*: 'Alias autem si intelligamus istud statutum loqui de ipsis fructibus beneficiorum vel portionum quovismodo non concedendis laico ad firmam, sic expresse contradiceret dicto c. *vestra* (c. 2, X. 3. 18), contra cuius tenorem non valeret statutum editum per inferiorem, qui legem superioris tollere non potest.'

[2] *Ibid.* p. 154, gl. ad v. *adjiciendo*: 'et verum est quod constitutiones legatinas non poterit archiepiscopus tollere, quia inferior non potest tollere legem superioris.'

[3] *Ibid.* p. 246, gl. ad v. *declarandum*: 'Ubi verba constitutionis vel statuti sunt ambigua vel obscura, tunc interpretatio erit ipsius qui statuit . . . et ubi tamen sunt satis clara et aperta, ut est videre in dicta constitutione Othoboni, tunc inferior praelatus potest declarare intellectum talis statuti, sicut alias solet notari per doctores, Extra, *de iudi.* c. *cum venissent* (c. 12, X. 2. 1). Vel dic quod ubi declaratio statuti est iuri consona, tunc bene tenet declaratio statuti facta per inferiorem, ut clare patet Extra, *de consue.* c. *cum dilectus* (c. 8, X. 1. 4). Ubi vero statutum est adeo obscurum quod non potest haberi congrua expositio, tunc recurrendum est ad statuentem.'

that its words are so plain that they need no interpreter. Then this same John Peckham has used another phrase that is not very apt. He has said, 'We order' that one of Ottobon's constitutions shall be inviolably observed. This, says Lyndwood, is 'executive,' not 'authoritative.' The statute came from one who had a higher authority than the archbishop had, so he could add no authority to it; still it is a useful practice to draw attention to existing laws, so that they may not be forgotten.[1]

Such is Lyndwood's comment on Peckham's action. Very different indeed is the comment on it which has been made in modern times. 'The provincial law of the Church of England contained, as has been stated, the constitutions of the archbishops from Langton downwards, and the canons passed in the legatine councils under Otho and Ottobon. The latter, which might possibly be treated as in themselves wanting the sanction of the national church, were ratified in councils held by Peckham.'[2] Now for the time we may leave open the question which of these two explanations is the truer expression of the mind of Peckham and his contemporaries; but as to the theory that prevailed in the court of Canterbury during Lyndwood's tenure of office there can be no doubt whatever. Peckham and his councils could not 'ratify' legatine constitutions. In such a context 'the sanction of the national church' = 0.

That as a matter of fact the English bishops did not enforce some of the decretals, even in cases in which

---

[1] Lyndwood, p. 11, gl. ad v. *observari* : 'Sed cum dicta constitutio Othoboni per ipsum qui erat maioris auctoritatis, quia per legatum a latere, erat edita et debite publicata . . . ad quid praecipitur hic dictam constitutionem observari, cum per prius sufficienter ligabat? Dic quod istud est praeceptum potius executivum illius quod primo statutum est quam auctoritativum, videlicet cum istud praeceptum est ad excitandum negligentes observare constitutionem ipsam. . . .'

[2] *Report of the Ecclesiastical Courts Commission*, vol. i. p. 25.

they could not urge the excuse that they **were prevented from** so **doing** by the **lay** power, **is highly** probable. John **of Ayton** in his grumbling gloss **says** that the only constitutions that are enforced **with any** alacrity are those **which** bring profit to episcopal **purses.**[1] Lyndwood in **his** preface says that the provincial constitutions have **been very generally neglected** by **prelates,** judges, **and others. Perhaps there are in our own day** some **portions of the law ecclesiastical which are not** being **rigorously executed. Our inquiry, however, is** whether **English canonists asserted any principle which would justify disobedience to papal constitutions. Let us hear Lyndwood about this matter.**

He gives us a constitution of Archbishop Peckham which prohibits nuns from remaining outside their cloisters, and which declares that those who break this edict are to be excommunicated. It seems, however, to admit certain exceptions. A nun is not to remain at large for more than three days for the sake of recreation, nor for more than six days for any cause, except infirmity, unless it be with the consent of the bishop. A saving clause deals with the case of those who are compelled to beg their bread. Now for the comment.

> Whatever this statute may say, the common law is that nuns ought to remain perpetually in cloister, and ought not to go out for any cause except for the two limited in [c. un. in Sexto, 3. 16, a decree which is there ascribed to Boniface VIII., and which allows a nun to be outside cloister if she is suffering from sickness, and permits an abbess or prioress to leave the house in order to do homage for a fief]. And therefore [says Lyndwood] this constitution [he means Peckham's] has but little effect, regard being had to the common law, which cannot be abrogated by the constitution of an inferior. If, then, you ask me what effect this constitution has, especially as its author, John Peckham, well knew that Bonifician constitution, I do not see a good answer, unless it be that perchance the constitution of Boniface had not been accepted

---

[1] Joh. de Athona, p. 37, gl. ad v. *et cappis clausis.*

and executed in England, as we may see with our own eyes to-day in many monasteries of nuns in England, and in that case this constitution [namely, Peckham's] may well proceed.[1]

There is more to come; but, pausing here for a moment, we may observe that Lyndwood is to all seeming dealing out hard measure to Peckham, by charging him with knowledge of a law that was not made until after his death. The decretal in question seems to be,[2] as Lyndwood thought it was, a decretal of Boniface VIII.; but whereas Boniface did not become pope until 1295, Peckham died in 1292. Let us, then, do this tardy act of justice to the memory of a maligned archbishop. He did not presume to reject decretals. That he should have done so can never have seemed very probable to those who read his constitutions, for the words which he used when speaking of the Council of Lyons seem to have been just such as would be expected of an inferior prelate by the strongest papalists of our own day. He told the assembled clergy that 'those whom Peter binds with the chains of his laws are bound in the palace of the supreme and heavenly Emperor.'[3] He then added

[1] Lyndwood, p. 212, gl. ad v. *cum socia*: 'Quicquid itaque hic statuatur, verum est de iure communi quod moniales remanere debent sub perpetua clausura, nec exire debent quovismodo, nisi in duobus casibus limitatis in c. unico. eo. ti. li. 6. Unus casus est . . . Secundus casus est . . . Et propterea constitutio ista modicam vim obtinet respectu iuris communis, quod tolli non potest per constitutionem inferioris : *de elec.* c. *ne Romani* in Cle. [c. 2, Clem. 1. 3]. Si igitur quaeras de quo operatur ista constitutio, maxime cum Io. Peecham auctor huius constitutionis bene noverat constitutionem illam Bonificianam, c. ti. l. 6, responsionem bonam non video, nisi quod illa constitutio Bonifacii forsan non erat acceptata in Anglia nec executa, prout in pluribus monasteriis monialium in Anglia hodie videmus ad oculum : unde in hoc casu bene procedit ista constitutio, quae disponit circa ipsarum egressum.' See Peckham's decree on this subject in his *Register*, i. 265, and Wilkins, *Concilia*, ii. 61.
[2] *C. J. Can.*, ed. Friedberg, ii. col. 1053.
[3] Const. Jo. Peckham, *Ab exordio*. . . . 'Quippe quos legum suarum Petrus ligat vinculis in summi et caelestis Imperatoris palatio sunt ligati. . . .' See also Wilkins, *Concilia*, ii. 51.

that **the** decrees **of** the recent Council **of** Lyons were being infringed. **Therefore,** and that **no** one might shield himself by a plea **of** ignorance, he willed that those decrees should be recapitulated ; **so** that not only might they become known to all, but also, **if there** should happen **to be in them** anything **incompatible with the** custom **of this** country (which in **many** points **differed** from the custom **of** all **other lands), some** temperament of them might be humbly **implored from the apostolic** clemency, since, **as** holy **scripture says, obedience is** better than sacrifice, and disobedience **was ruining the** English church.[1] Then **Ottobon's constitutions were to** be read, and **this the more reverently because Ottobon** himself **had ordered that they should be recited once a year. Then the constitutions of Archbishop Boniface's council were to be read, and the question whether they were to be enforced was to be discussed, since it was said that an appeal (an appeal to the pope) had been made against them.**[2] **Lastly, Peckham was going to add some ordinances of his own. Now, surely all** this **would be scrupulously correct language in the mouth of a Roman Catholic archbishop at the present time.**

[1] 'Et quia Lugdunense concilium ultimo celebratum eo enormius quo recentius infringitur : ne quis possit se de temeritate huiusmodi per ignorantiam excusare, ipsum volumus in principio recenseri, ut non solum omnibus innotescat, verum etiam si quid in ipso videatur intolerabile istius consuetudini regionis, quae in multis ab omnibus aliis est distincta, circa [*al.* contra] illud temperamentum apostolicae clementiae humiliter imploretur, quoniam sacro testante eloquio, melior est obedientia quam victima, et quasi peccatum ariolandi est repugnare et quasi scelus [*al.* zelus] est idolatriae nolle acquiescere. Hanc enim inobedientiam credimus esse causam mutationis miserabilis utriusque parietis ecclesiae Anglicanae.' Peckham seems to have made strenuous efforts to enforce the decrees of the Council of Lyons ; see Peckham's *Register*, i. 137, 143, 257, etc.

[2] ' Tertio vero recitari volumus concilium de Lambeth, quod sanctae memoriae praedecessor noster Bonifacius cum fratribus et coepiscopis sui temporis noscitur salubriter edidisse, ut circa [*al.* contra] ipsum, quod dicitur fuisse appellatione suspensum, qualiter procedi debeat videatur.'

When Blessed Peter makes laws for England which do not seem to be suited to our climate, it is the right and duty of his subordinates in this country 'humbly to implore the apostolic clemency for a temperament.' But if Blessed Peter will not temper his laws, then 'obedience is better than sacrifice.'[1]

No, Lyndwood was hasty, and Peckham was the last man against whom he ought to have brought this accusation. In a letter addressed to Edward I.,[2] which breathes the spirit of the as yet unissued *Unam sanctam*, the archbishop told the king that the Emperor of all has given authority to the decrees of the popes, and that all men, all kings, are bound by those decrees. Boniface VIII. could add little to this letter when he declared, affirmed, and defined that it is necessary to the salvation of every human being to be subject to the Roman pontiff.

But, to return to the nuns, whatever Peckham may have done or wished to do, Lyndwood holds that the law must now be found in the Sext. The nuns, it seems, are not observing even Peckham's too indulgent rule. Why so? 'I cannot tell,' says Lyndwood, 'unless

---

[1] 'It may be that the legislature legislating for the whole catholic world may command a something that would not be adapted to the circumstances of every country. The bishops of those countries would be at liberty to represent respectfully to the holy father that the constitution did not suit the circumstances of their country, and in all such cases he would give an exemption; that is what he would ordinarily do. . . . But if he insisted, if he said, "I have received your representations, and I do not think them of sufficient weight to exempt your country; I require you to put this constitution in force," they would have no alternative but to accept it and put it in force.' This comes from the evidence given in 1873 by the Archbishop of Cashel in the O'Keeffe case; see *Report*, by H. C. Kirkpatrick (Longmans, 1874), at p. 502. See also Hinschius, *Kirchenrecht*, iii. 785. By Roman Catholic canonists of our own century it has been asserted and denied that in such a case a bishop would be justified in declining to enforce the new rule while the pope was being consulted.

[2] Peckham's *Register*, i. 239.

this be due to the lukewarmness of the bishops. You
ought to consider,' he adds, 'that the injunction in the
Sext is directed to the bishops who have nuns under
them, also to the abbots, exempt and non-exempt, to
whom some nuns are subject. But in truth in England
those nuns who are ruled by the "religious" are cloistered,
whilst those who are immediately under the bishops are
not cloistered, and so it is apparent that the negligence in
this matter lies with the bishops; and the bishops cannot
aid themselves against this law by prescription, as the
archdeacon (Guido de Baysio) notes.' In short, if the
law laid down in the Sext is not being enforced, the
bishops are to blame, for this is not one of the limited
class of rules which can be deprived of their power by
long-continued non-observance.[1]

Occasionally the canonists will use language which
at first sight may seem to imply that a law derives its
binding force from its 'acceptance' by those to whom it
is addressed, and that therefore a statute which has not
been thus accepted 'does not bind.' The canonists, most
unfortunately for them, have started with some muddled
definitions which apparently teach that a *lex* is confirmed
moribus utentium.[2] But when they come to practical
questions their talk about acceptance and approbation
seems to mean no more than that in certain cases a
judge ought to hold that a statute has lost its force by
non-observance and has thus fallen into desuetude.
There is a constitution of Ottobon declaring that the

[1] Lyndwood, p. 212, gl. ad v. *cum socia* : 'Considerare enim debes quod iniunctio illius capituli *periculoso* dirigitur episcopis quibus subsunt huiusmodi moniales . . . et sic apparet quod negligentia circa hoc remansit in episcopis, nec potest contra illud ius praescribi, prout ibi notat Archidiaconus.'

[2] Dictum Gratiani post c. 3, Dist. 4 : 'Leges instituuntur cum promulgantur, firmantur cum moribus utentium approbantur. Sicut enim moribus utentium in contrarium nonnullae leges hodie abrogatae sunt, ita moribus utentium ipsae leges confirmantur.'

archbishops and bishops are not to delegate causes except to men holding certain official positions in the church. There is a constitution of Otto about the dress of the clergy. Both John of Ayton and Lyndwood are for holding that these constitutions are not binding, because they have not been accepted.[1] By this they seem to mean no more than that these old laws have been so much ignored that they are no longer to be enforced. This doctrine of desuetude is limited in various ways. It will only be applied to a law about matters that are morally indifferent, to a law that does not execute itself by means of a *sententia lata*, and to a law that does not expressly prohibit the contrary of that practice which it enjoins; and far from our canonists is the thought that the subjects of the legislator may lawfully conspire to refuse the statutes that he sets upon them.

We have been speaking as though the provincial legislation proceeded from the archbishop, not from the provincial council. This is Lyndwood's strain throughout his book. The archbishop makes statutes for his suffragans and his other subjects (*subditi*).[2] True that he should undertake no *ardua negotia* without the counsel of his brethren; *consilio fratrum nostrorum*, or some similar phrase, should occur in his constitutions.[3] Still he is the legislator. Thus a collision between a provincial constitution and a decretal would not be a collision between two 'churches,' an English church and a foreign church; it would be simply a collision between an 'inferior' and a 'superior,' between *subditus* and *princeps*.

---

[1] Joh. de Athon, p. 37, gl. ad v. *et cappis clausis*; p. 123, gl. ad v *committantur*. Lyndwood, p. 80, gl. ad v. *viris discretis*; p. 118, gl. ad v. *cappis clausis*.

[2] See, e.g., Lyndwood, p. 32, gl. ad v. *nostrae iurisdictioni*.

[3] Lyndwood, p. 104, gl. ad v. *fratrum nostrorum consilio*. See also Joh. de Athon, p. 5, gl. ad v. *et consensu*.

As we should expect, it is rarely that Lyndwood finds any discrepancy between the archiepiscopal constitutions and the system of the *ius commune*. It is, we may say, his duty to harmonise them. The statutes of the inferior legislator ought to be so construed that they may not conflict with the statutes of the superior. For example, a decretal of Boniface VIII., which stands in the Sext, ordains that a monk is not to act as a testamentary executor without the consent of his superior—that is, his abbot. But Archbishop Peckham has said that a monk is not to act as a testamentary executor without the consent of the ordinary. These two precepts may well be read together; both consents must be obtained. Lyndwood, however, cannot tell us this without repeating once more that provincial legislation cannot derogate from that *ius papale* which is the common law of the church.[1] A natural desire to magnify his office would have led him to expand rather than to contract the sphere allowed to the legislation of the metropolitan whose representative he was; but to all seeming, this impulse he does not feel, or resists. It cannot prevail against his science, and his science is cosmopolitan and papal. If there be conflict, or apparent conflict, the words of the provincial statute must be whittled away, not the words of the decretal.

There are other cases in which Lyndwood expresses an outspokenly unfavourable opinion touching some of the archiepiscopal statutes, and this in a book which

---

[1] Lyndwood, p. 168, gl. ad v. *ordinariorum*: 'Requiritur enim licentia abbatis, ut patet in d. c. *Religiosus* [c. 2 in Sexto, 3. 11]. . . . Requiritur etiam licentia ordinarii ex vigore huius statuti, quod in hoc non derogat iuri papali sed accumulat, et hoc satis licet, ut notant Hostiensis et Iohannes.' Gl. ad v. *permittatur*: 'Quod capitulum [c. 2 in Sexto, 3. 11] cum ius commune contineat, huic constitutioni, in quantum per eam illi iuri obviari posset, debet praeferri, maxime cum inferior legi superioris derogare non poterit.' It seems possible that here again Lyndwood has forgotten Peckham's date.

with many pretty words he will dedicate to Archbishop Chichele. Of one statute he says that he thinks it cannot be a provincial, but can only be a synodal constitution, 'because in several points, so it seems to me, it is contrary to the fundamental principles of law.'[1] On another occasion he tells us that he is going to examine one of Peckham's constitutions carefully, for Peckham was a friar and may be suspected of unduly favouring his fellow friars.[2] In a third case Stratford has decreed that his suffragans are not to have more than a certain number of apparitors, and has seemingly added that any apparitors appointed in breach of this rule are *ipso facto* suspended from the office of apparitor for ever. Whereupon Lyndwood says: 'It seems to me that this punishment is irregular, for an apparitor entering on the office by the appointment of his superior commits no offence, and where there is no offence there ought to be no punishment.'[3] If there is any passage in which Lyndwood speaks in a similar tone of a decretal, I have missed it.[4] It is not for a lawyer who is writing a practical law-book to criticise the edicts of a sovereign legislature, however bad they may be; but the edicts of a non-sovereign legislature he must criticise, for they may well be so bad as to be invalid.

Lyndwood's task, however, is not very hard. On the whole the archbishops have kept their statutes well

---

[1] Lyndwood, p. 19, gl. ad v. *synodali*: 'Nec puto hanc [constitutionem] processisse de decreto provincialis [concilii], quia in pluribus, ut mihi videtur, est contra fundamenta legum et iurium.'

[2] *Ibid.* p. 228, gl. ad v. *socios sacerdotes.*

[3] *Ibid.* p. 226, gl. ad v. *perpetuo*: 'Mihi videtur quod illa poena est irregularis.'

[4] In quoting from an old writer he sometimes gives a passage which tells of a time when the school of canonists still spoke of decretals with some freedom: *e.g.* p. 297, gl. ad v. *ordinarii*: 'Nec obstat secundum eum Hostiensem quod textus ibi dicit *a Sede Apostolica delegatis*, quia hoc dixit papa ut placeret exemptis, secundum eum.'

within the limits that are set by the catholic system. The series of provincial constitutions on which he comments covers a period of two centuries. But we have here no great bulk of law. It is a small thing to put beside the Sext, which represents some sixty years of papal activity. When, as Lyndwood does, we have cut away from the constitutions their preambles or harangues, what is left is by no means a weighty mass. Be it granted that the importance of a law is not to be measured by its length; but, if we turn from quantity to quality, the more carefully we examine these constitutions from Lyndwood's point of view, the lower will be our estimate of their importance. They are essentially 'bye-laws' in the modern sense of that term. In Lyndwood's eyes some of them do nothing at all, or very little; they are but the provincial publication of law that was already binding on all the faithful. This publication of existing rules, if humble, is still useful work; it deprives the offender of any hope that he may have of pleading his ignorance of the edict that he infringes. Also in the middle ages even the canons of a general council will but slowly penetrate to country rectories, unless the provincial prelates bestir themselves. There are, again, special reasons for re-enacting old law which might not occur to the mind of a modern layman. Whereas a secular legislator is content if he can punish those who break his edicts, the church desires to legislate not only for the *forum externum* but for the *forum internum* also. She does not merely want to punish those who break her laws; she wishes to be able to say that they have sinned in breaking them. She can control the procedure of her public courts, but she can also control the procedure of the confessional. Now in the *forum internum* we can hardly assert that ignorance of a rule is never an excuse for breaking it. Hence a more than usually strong desire on the part of ecclesiastical legislators to deprive their subjects of the plea of ignorance.[1] In the second place, an archbishop by re-enacting an old law as a provincial constitution is, as Lyndwood explains to us, amplifying his jurisdiction. If a subject of one of the suffragan bishops breaks a provincial constitution, the archbishop can punish the offender, and a case which under the common law would have gone to the diocesan court may thus be brought before the archbishop's official.[2]

Then, again (to recur to the character of the constitutions), there are numerous cases in which the breakers of some rule of common law are threatened with a new statutory punishment. This is legitimate work for provincial councils. They ought to enforce the *ius commune*, and, if need be, to arm it with new penalties. Energy enough has been spent by Boniface of Savoy and his suffragans in proclaiming against the state the liberties of the church. This, when regarded from the canonist's standpoint, is laudable energy; but Lyndwood has to confess that it has been spent in vain. The constitutions of Boniface are so little observed that they are hardly worthy of a gloss.[3] For the rest, very little has been done; for very little could be done. We should be exceedingly unjust to Peckham and Winchelsea if we set their constitutions beside the statutes of Edward I. It was not for them to be trenchant or drastic; it was not for them to be original. They could

---

[1] See, *e.g.*, the discussion by Lyndwood, p. 11, gl. ad v. *observari*, of the question whether a man sins mortally by infringing a constitution.

[2] Lyndwood, pp. 239, 240, gl. ad v. *competentem*.

[3] *Ibid.* p. 92, gl. ad v. *contingit aliquando*: 'Istud est statutum Bonifacii archiepiscopi, prout sunt plura alia in hoc libro inserta : et pro maiori parte constitutiones ipsius Bonifacii sunt poenales et concernunt libertatem ecclesiasticam et eius violationem. Sed quia in paucis servantur hae constitutiones, ideo circa earum glossationem brevius pertranseo.'

not imitate *Quia emptores* or the Statute of Mortmain. They were 'inferior' legislators, and this at a time when their superiors were legislating profusely. That many of these provincial constitutions did good, that they were the outcome of a zealous desire to correct faults and remove abuses, we may be very ready to admit; but, when we look at them through the eyes of the English canonist, we see that they contain little that is new, and are only a brief appendix to the common law of the universal church.

If for a moment we were to regard these provincial constitutions as forming the whole or the main part of the ecclesiastical law that was administered in England, we should stand amazed at their meagreness. This would be forced upon our notice by Lyndwood's procedure. He arranges them according to the plan adopted by Bernard of Pavia in the Compilatio Prima and sanctioned by Gregory IX. Of course we must have five books, no more, no less—*iudex, iudicium, clerus, sponsalia, crimen*. Then in each book we must have as many as possible of the Gregorian titles. Thus we shall begin with *De Summa Trinitate*, and end with *De Verborum Significatione*, since our constitutions will not afford us even one little text that would bear the title *De Regulis Iuris*. This is the convenient arrangement for a book that is to be ancillary to the Decretals. Lyndwood will try to make as many titles as possible. But, do all he can, he can make only 75, while Gregory has 185. In other words, the commentator finds that nothing has been said by English legislators touching more than half of the recognised topics of ecclesiastical jurisprudence. Yet he does his best to multiply titles. Thus he will have a rubric *De Homicidio*; it will look well. But what can be put under it? First, a constitution of Archbishop Edmund which enjoins that the living child shall be cut from the body of the dead mother; secondly, a constitution which merely declares that a certain rule has been established by the fourth Lateran Council, and is to be frequently proclaimed in church—namely, the rule that if the patron of a church kills or mutilates the rector, vicar, or clerk, he is to forfeit the patronage, and his posterity to the fourth generation are not to be received into a religious house.[1] This is poor stuff of which to make a title *De Homicidio*, poor stuff to set beside the parallel title in Pope Gregory's book, which contains a wealth of texts about voluntary and involuntary homicide. Yet an English ecclesiastical court may any day have before it a clerk accused of having slain his neighbour, and will have to decide whether he is punishable or no. One thing is clear: such a clerk will not be judged out of the provincial constitutions.

Then let us look at the fourth book, the book on marriage. That book contains in all four chapters. The parallel book in the Decretals contains 166. Now marriage is not a matter that can be left to judicial discretion or natural equity. It is pre-eminently a matter about which there must be hard and fast rules. In the middle ages the rules were but too numerous, but too intricate. Suppose that we want to know the English marriage law. We shall certainly not find it, or any appreciable part of it, in the four texts that Lyndwood has collected. The first draws attention to the legislation of the fourth Lateran Council concerning banns,[2] makes it a little more precise, and adds that priests are to enjoin the faithful not to enter into secret marriage engagements. The second, which deals with the espousals of children, is simply an old decretal em-

---

[1] c. 12, X. 5. 37.   [2] c. 3, X. 4. 3.

bodying a text from the Decretum.¹ The third returns to the subject of banns, and directs the bishops to cause the decretal *Cum inhibitio* (a canon of the fourth Lateran Council²) to be expounded in the vulgar tongue, and observed by all priests, whether they be parish priests or no, under pain of suspension for three years. In several respects the rules about this matter seem to have been made a little more severe against the priests; but the substance of the marriage law is left untouched. The fourth constitution adds the greater excommunication to all the other penalties incurred by men or women who contract marriage when they are aware of an impediment, and by priests who, without due licence, celebrate marriage between non-parishioners, or who celebrate clandestine marriages procured by force or fear. Now all this may be very useful, but it is not the law of marriage; it is a little penal supplement to the law of marriage. No one knew that better than Lyndwood, and so he has told us where to look for the law of marriage. At the opening of his fourth book he writes thus:—

Here we might discuss what is marriage, whence it derives its name, how it is contracted, where it was instituted, what are the causes of its institution, what good flows from it, and what impediments there are to it. Of all these matters Innocentius has treated, and yet more fully Johannes Andreae.³

In other words, there is no English law of marriage. If you want to know whether you are old enough to marry, whether you may marry your late wife's second cousin or your godmother's daughter, whether a religious ceremony is essential to a marriage, whether you have good cause for a divorce, you will

---

[1] c. un. C. 30. qu. 2; c. 2. X. 4. 2. The slight variations in the language (such as *urgente* for *urgentissima*) are probably not intentional.
[2] c. 3. X. 4. 3.   [3] Lyndwood, p. 271, gl. ad v. *matrimonium*.

find your answer in the *ius commune* of the church, and, in order to start you upon your investigations, I refer you to the works of two Italian canonists of high repute, one of whom was a layman, the other a pope.

The general notion that we obtain from Lyndwood's book about the theory of law dominant in our English courts will be strengthened if we turn to the *Pupilla Oculi*.[1] That little manual seems to have been compiled by John de Burgh in 1385, at a time when he was chancellor of the university of Cambridge. It was meant to be an elementary book; it was designed rather for priests than for professed students of the law. There is not much argument in it. The main rules of ecclesiastical law are briefly and dogmatically expounded. Notice is taken of the legatine and of the provincial constitutions, but a subordinate position is assigned to them. For example, John first states all the cases that he can remember in which a man is excommunicated by the general law of the church, and then turns to the cases in which the legatine and provincial constitutions impose that penalty.[2] The idea which seems to govern his procedure is that the *ius commune*, the general law of the church, is eked out at a few points by purely English ordinances. About many of the topics that he touches, notably the elaborate law of marriage, these English ordinances are absolutely silent. There is no talk of setting English practice against Italian theory. About many a matter, great and small, there is no law except the law that is to be found in the decretals. Even the purely practical knowledge which will be

---

[1] *Pupilla Oculi* . . . edita impensis . . . Wilhelmi Bretton, with a prefatory letter, dated prid. kal. Feb. 1510. The book purports to have been written in 1385. In 1384 John de Burgh was confirmed as chancellor of the university (Cooper, *Annals of Cambridge*, i. 128).

[2] *Pupilla Oculi*, f. 55.

useful to the parish priest must be a knowledge of rules which have no other source than the legislative power of the popes.

And if the English provinces had but little enacted law that was all their own, they had also but little customary law that derogated from the *ius commune*. Of custom the canonist, like every other medieval lawyer, will speak civil words; but when it comes to a practical question he is by no means willing to admit that a custom excludes those general rules which he is in the habit of applying. Like his brethren of the temporal courts he has been engaged in a grand work of unification and centralisation; and so he is wont to throw on the custom a duty of strict proof. In the first place, it must show itself to be a *consuetudo praescripta*, one that has gained its right to exist by existing for a long space of time.[1] Secondly, it must be reasonable, and its reasonableness will be judged by men who are professionally convinced of the reasonableness of the rule from which it purports to be an exception. In the details of divine service there was, indeed, a considerable room for variety.[2] A long-continued custom, says Lyndwood, sanctions 'the use' of Salisbury throughout the province of Canterbury, though according to the *ius commune* 'the use' of the metropolitan church should be the model.[3] But the possibility of disputes about ritual did not fill any large space in the mind of the canonist, who had many other things to think about, and outside the ritualistic sphere we read of little law that has its base in distinctively English custom. It is not an important rule that after Lady Day a rector has power to

[1] Lyndwood, p. 25, gl. ad v. *de consuetudine*: 'Nam verbum consuetudinis simpliciter prolatum intelligitur de praescripta ... maxime cum sit contra ius commune.'
[2] *Ibid.* p. 102, gl. ad v. *Thomae Martyris*.
[3] *Ibid.* p. 104, gl. ad v. *Usum Sarum*.

dispose of the tithes which will become due at the next harvest; but, as this English rule conflicts with the common law, Lyndwood has to argue that it is not unreasonable, to cite the doctors and allege an analogous rule that is to be found in the feudal law of Lombardy.[1] The two really important English customs of which we hear are that which, diverging from the *ius commune*, imposes on the parishioners, and not on the rector, the burden of maintaining the nave of the parish church,[2] and that which assigns to the spiritual courts an exclusive jurisdiction in testamentary causes, and thus gives the canonist more than he can ask for in the name of his *ius commune*.[3] It were needless to say that he thinks these customs eminently reasonable. On the other hand, a custom to pay no tithes would be bad,[4] and, when the temporal judges begin to talk of custom in defence of their usurpations, then is brought into play the text in the Decretum which tells us how Christ said not 'I am the custom,' but 'I am the truth.'[5] But (to leave the ground that is debated between church and state) it will be sufficiently plain that the ecclesiastical law that Lyndwood administered in his court was only in a very slight measure law which in his eyes traced its source to English customs, and that an advocate would hardly have persuaded him to enforce any usage which departed from 'the common law' unless some words of Innocentius or Hostiensis or Johannes Andreae which expressly left room for such a custom could have been produced.

It is probable enough that in the inferior courts,

---

[1] Lyndwood, p. 25, gl. ad v. *de consuetudine*. He cites 'Auth. *hic finitur lex*, § *si vasallus*, col. decima.' The reference is to Feud. lib. 2, tit. 28, § 2.
[2] *Ibid.* p. 53, gl. ad v. *reparatione*.
[3] *Ibid.* p. 170, gl. ad v. *insinuationem*.
[4] *Ibid.* p. 190, gl. ad v. *arbitrantur*; p. 192, gl. ad v. *consuetudines*.
[5] c. 5, Dist. 8.

the courts of archdeacons and rural deans, a law was administered that might in some sort be called customary, since its main rule was the rule of thumb. Lyndwood tells us that the rural deans are usually ignorant of the law,[1] and that the officials of the archdeacons are but moderately learned.[2] He thinks that a three years' study of the law may perhaps be enough to qualify a man to practise as an advocate in the petty courts, since important cases are not heard there.[3] Ruridecanal law may have stood on a level with crowner's quest law, and no doubt the church had her Shallows and her Silences. In inferior courts you will get inferior law. But crowner's quest law did not profess a right to be something other than king's bench law; to the best of its poor ability it would attempt to be the law of Westminster Hall. Even so we may believe that the archidiaconal and episcopal officials, though their libraries would be very small when compared with the store of ancient and modern books that Lyndwood perused, did the best they could to make their law as good as that which prevailed in the metropolitan court. In most cases their sentences were subject to appeal, and, if they were ambitious men, they might hope that some day a reputation for learning would secure their promotion to a higher seat. But at any rate of an endeavour to set up a schismatical law of their own we must hold them guiltless, until so serious a charge has been seriously made. We must concern ourselves rather with the ideal that our spiritual judges kept before their minds than with the results that they achieved. For ignor-

---

[1] Lyndwood, p. 79, gl. ad v. *audire praesumant*: 'quia, ut communiter, tales decani rurales sunt imperiti et iuris ignari.'

[2] *Ibid.* p. 81, gl. ad v. *committatur*: 'tales officiales modicam peritiam in iure habent.' In the previous sentence *Archiepiscopus* should be *Archidiaconus*.

[3] *Ibid.* p. 76, gl. ad v. *per triennium*.

ance, stupidity, perversity, some allowance, and perhaps a large allowance, must be made; but that judges should be ignorant, stupid, perverse, can never be a legal principle.

Again, we shall not find in Lyndwood's book any English 'case law,' any 'case law' of our English ecclesiastical courts. If any decisions are referred to, they will be decisions of the Rota.[1] Had his glosses come down to us without the text that they enshrine, we might have read page after page without finding any proof of his Englishry. What his predecessors in the provincial court may have done has no interest for him; their judgments are not for one moment to be set beside the Sext or the Clementines, or even beside the opinions of 'the doctors,' the French and Italian doctors, William de Montlezun and Henry de Bohic, Petrus de Ancharano and Antonius de Butrio. His science was a science to which for two centuries past Englishmen had added next to nothing, but which they had dutifully accepted at the hands of foreigners. And yet he belonged to a nation which was producing the Year Books and the most thoroughly national system of temporal law that the medieval world could show. But whereas the English state was an independent whole, the English church was in the eyes of its own judges a dependent fragment whose laws had been imposed upon it from without.

It seems to me, then, that if Lyndwood had been

---

[1] Lyndwood, p. 78: 'Et hoc modo procedit dictum Dominorum de Rota in conclusione 63 et 64'; p. 82: 'Et hoc tenent Domini de Rota sua conclusione 328 et sua conclusione 309'; p. 118: 'Et haec est conclusio Dominorum de Rota conclusione 562'; p. 144: 'Sed Domini de Rota conclusione 168 (al. 188) dicunt'; p. 147: 'Dominicus [de Sancto Geminiano] . . . dicit quod sic, et hoc tenent, ut asserit, Domini de Rota conclusione 301.' Joh. de Athona, p. 17: 'Et sic fertur determinatum per omnes auditores palatii contra religiosos Sancti Bartholomaei Londinensis.'

asked **whether** 'the canon law of Rome' was binding upon him and the other ecclesiastical judges in England, he would in the first **place** have excepted to the form of **the question.** He would have said something of this kind :—

I do not quite understand what you mean by 'the canon **law of Rome.'** If you mean thereby any **rules** which relate only to the diocese of which the pope is bishop, or to the province of which the pope is metropolitan, then it is obvious enough that we in England have not to administer the canon law of Rome. But even if this be **your** meaning, you must be careful to avoid a mistake. I, whatever **else** I may be, am the official of a papal legate ; the archiepiscopal court, over which I preside, is the court of a papal legate. It is the duty of a legatine court to copy as nearly as may be the procedure of the Roman court. The *mos et stylus Curiae Romanae* are my models. They are my excuse, or rather my warrant, if, for example, I cite any of the archbishop's *subditi* to appear before him 'wheresoever he shall be within his province,' without naming any particular place for their appearance. In so doing, I am exercising a legatine and Roman privilege, and am administering specifically Roman rules.[1] However, I very much fear that this is not your meaning, that what you call the canon law of Rome is what I call the *ius commune* of the church, and that you are hinting that I am not bound by the statutes that the popes have decreed for all the faithful. If that be so, I must tell you that your hint is not only erroneous but heretical. That you will withdraw it I hope and believe, for otherwise, though we are sincerely sorry when we are driven to extremities, the archbishop may feel it his painful duty to relinquish you to the lay arm, and you know what follows relinquishment.[2] Your case, though sad, is not unprecedented. The test that I must exact of you and others suspected of Lollardy has

---

[1] Lyndwood, p. 82, gl. ad v. *loco*: 'Pro investigatione veritatis huius quaesiti debes scire quod archiepiscopus Cantuariensis est legatus sedis apostolicae natus, sicut legitur (c. 1, X. 1. 30). Et ad legatos dicti sedis spectat ut in citationibus et aliis formis sequantur stylum curiae Romanae . . . et quod mos curiae Romanae sequendus est notatur bene per Hostiensem, . . . et ad legatum pertinet in citationibus se conformare stylo curiae Romanae, quod ad instar papae, cuius vices gerit, poterit ad locum indeterminatum citare.'

[2] Lyndwood, p. 296, gl. ad v. *sententialiter declaretur*, shows an honourable desire to save even the relapsed heretic from the flames. But still law is law.

been already formulated. It is this: you must declare that every Christian is bound to obey all the constitutions and ordinances contained in the Decretum, the Decretals, the Sext, and the Clementines, in such wise as obedience is demanded for them by the Roman Church.[1]

Though even as an exercise of historical imagination, we have no wish to see divers reverend, noble, and learned commissioners playing the passive part in an 'act of faith,' we must look at one more sentence in the famous Report:—

> The constitutions of the archbishops, from Stephen Langton downwards, and the canons passed in legatine councils under Otho and Ottobon, ratified by the national church under Archbishop Peckham, were finally received as the texts of English church law, under the hands of the commentators, John of Ayton and William Lyndwood. These commentators introduced into their notes large extracts from and references to both the canon and civil law of Rome, but these were not a part of the authoritative jurisprudence.[2]

That this may be true of what happened 'finally' is very possible, for the world did not come to an end at the Reformation. Nor can anyone dispute that the legatine and provincial constitutions were the most important 'texts of English church law,' if by English church law be meant that part of the law administered in the English church courts which was merely English. Nor, again, is any statutory authority to be attributed to the notes of our two glossators; they are but the notes of learned men. Lastly, I believe that they would have been quite content to put the civil law of Rome, the law of Justinian's books, on a pretty low level. Lyndwood advises the young canonist to study only

---

[1] See the test applied to Richard Wyche, *Fasciculi Zizaniorum*, 504. As to his trial, see *Report of the Ecclesiastical Courts Commission*, 1883, vol. i. p. 61.

[2] *Report of the Ecclesiastical Courts Commission*, 1883, vol. i. p. xviii.

such portions of the *ius civile* as are referred to in the gloss on the canon law;[1] and John of Ayton lays down what seems to have been the orthodox doctrine when he says that a *lex imperialis* which favours the church is to be received, unless it has been rejected by the apostolic see, while a *lex imperialis* which makes against the church is to be rejected, unless the apostolic see has approved it.[2] But, for all this, the contrast between the royal commissioners and Lyndwood is startling. The last is put first and the first last; the inferior prelate takes the place of the pope. In Lyndwood's view the decretals are not merely 'a part of the authoritative jurisprudence,' but its supremely authoritative part. Next in order of rank stand the legatine constitutions. To the third place we admit the provincial **constitutions,** provided that they do not contravene the laws **enacted** by popes or legates *a latere*. If Lyndwood had supposed that the *Provinciale* would serve as a manual for **those** who had inverted this natural order, he would **have** said —so it seems to me—that the end **not** merely **of** all sound theology, but of all rational **jurisprudence,** was at hand, and sooner than take **an** unwilling part in the impending catastrophe, he would **have** burnt his **book.**

Those, therefore, who maintain that the English ecclesiastical courts held themselves **free to** accept **or reject** the laws that were found *in corpore Decretorum et Decretalium*,[3] should be **prepared to treat Lyndwood's book as an exception, an aberration;** for what we find there **is a stark papalism, which leaves little enough**

---

[1] Lyndwood, p. 76, gl. ad v. *et civile*: 'Puto quod **sufficit quod talis** audiverit **ius** civile **secundum remissiones quae ponuntur in** glossa **iuris** canonici, **et sine** quibus iura canonica, **praesertim in** iudicialibus, **non possunt** bene intelligi nec sciri.'

[2] Joh. de **Athon**, pp. 76, 77.

[3] Lyndwood uses this **phrase on p. 147, gl. ad v.** *primitus amoveri*.

room for local custom, and absolutely no room for any liberties of the Anglican church which can be upheld against the law-giving power of the pope. Now we must not judge a school by a single book, even though it be almost the only book that the school produces, and we must not judge a long age by one critical moment. The extremest of Lyndwood's opinions may perhaps have been shared by few. We may believe that in 1430 there were many Englishmen, and some English canonists, who would openly and as a matter of principle have taken the part of a general council against a pope. Also it may be true that, owing to one cause and another, the time at which Lyndwood wrote was the time of all times at which orthodox Englishmen were papally minded. A discussion of these matters might take us far afield, and would, so I think, be irrelevant in the present context. Let us lay very little stress upon anything in Lyndwood's book that bears on the great open question of his day. About such a question a man's opinion, a nation's opinion, will be determined by multifarious forces and, it may be, by motives that are none the less urgent because they are not avowed — by international jealousies, party struggles, court intrigues.[1] Also we may remember that in the fifteenth century a lawyer might prostrate himself before the papal omnipotence and yet mean but little by the more extravagant of his phrases. The less the popes could do in the world of fact, the larger were the powers that might be safely attributed to them by theorists who were in search of that juristic desideratum, an all-competent sovereign. Our canonists

---

[1] Gascoigne (*Loci e Libro Veritatum*, p. 17) charges with inconsistency the bishops who supported Chichele in his resistance. They had been saying that every pope is above a general council; then they turned round and said plainly that a general council is above the pope.

obtain an intellectual luxury at a cheap rate when they place the *plenitudo potestatis* in a pope whose bulls, if like to be troublesome, will never reach their hands, but will be impounded by a secular power for whose doings they are not responsible. But what we ought to study if we would know our ecclesiastical courts, is the method and scheme of Lyndwood's book, more especially the theory that it applies when it determines the comparative authority of provincial constitutions and papal decretals. Here, if anywhere, we ought to see professional tradition, the tradition of the court over which Lyndwood presides; for questions about the relation borne to each other by the various sources of law must be frequently taking concrete shapes and crying aloud for decision. Of course it is just possible that even here Lyndwood is innovating, that he is attacking the general opinion of his predecessors or turning it inside out. If so, he is accomplishing his revolutionary design in a marvellously cool and dispassionate manner. The *Provinciale* does not wear the air of a book that is assailing old beliefs or a rooted course of practice. Nothing could be less polemical. It seems even to shirk the burning points of current controversy. Lyndwood is writing an elementary lawbook for beginners, and it is not in any argumentative disquisitions about legislative power but in the practical solution of everyday problems that his absolute submission to the *ius papale* becomes patent. He does not set himself to demonstrate in solemn form that an English council cannot derogate even from a legatine constitution; it does not seem to enter his head that anyone will dispute so self-evident a proposition.

But the time for a defence of Lyndwood's legal orthodoxy will have come when his heterodoxy—that is, his departure from an established Anglican tradition

—has been asserted. In the meantime I cannot but think that his work casts a heavy burden of proof upon the theory which would paint our English ecclesiastical courts selecting the decretals that they will accept, or which would ascribe to the three papal law-books 'great authority' indeed, but no statutory force. Has that burden of proof ever been borne? Has an attempt been made to bear it?

II. CHURCH, STATE, AND DECRETALS

In much of what has been written by historians and said by judges touching the fate of 'the Roman' or 'the foreign' canon law in England there seems to me to be a tendency towards the confusion of two propositions. The first is this: that in England the state did not suffer the church to appropriate certain considerable portions of that wide field of jurisdiction which the canonists claimed as the heritage of ecclesiastical law. The second is this: that the English courts Christian held themselves free to accept or reject, and did in some cases reject, 'the canon law of Rome.' The truth of the first proposition no one doubts; the truth of the second seems to me exceedingly dubious. At any rate we have here two independent propositions, and we do not prove the second by proving the first. The one deals with the extent of the field occupied and cultivated by ecclesiastical justice, the other with the course of agriculture. By proving that at the present time and in our own country the bishops of the Roman church have nothing that ought to be called jurisdiction, we should not prove that they do not think themselves bound by the canon law of Rome, nor even should we prove that they are not inducing their flocks to obey that law. To take another illustration, we must neither praise nor blame the English church for the law of divorce that is being administered to-day in the High Court of Justice, though not very long ago all matrimonial causes belonged to the spiritual forum. We must not attribute to the church what is done by the state. Is it not even possible that the submissiveness of the ecclesiastical courts to the canon law of Rome varied directly rather than inversely with the strength and aggressiveness of their secular rivals?

An example of the facile transitions that are made from the one to the other proposition I will take from the first place to which we should all look if we would learn anything about the law of the English church in the middle ages. I need not say that I mean the Historical Appendix which Dr. Stubbs added to the 'Report of the Ecclesiastical Courts Commission,' nor need I say that I regard that discourse with reverence and admiration. In it there is a section entitled *The Law Administered in the Courts of the English Church between the Conquest and the Reformation*.[1] That is the very matter about which we would fain know something; but we mentally underline the word *Church*. For a while all goes well. We find a strong statement of my second proposition. The papal law-books were regarded 'as manuals, but not as codes of statutes.' 'Attempts to force on the church and nation [again we underline the word *church*] the complete canon law of the middle ages were always unsuccessful.' No doubt, we say to ourselves, some proof, some illustration of this will come. We approach yet nearer to the focus.

> The laws which guided the English courts up to the time of the Reformation may, then, be thus arranged: (1) the canon law of Rome, comprising the decretum of Gratian; the decretals of Gregory IX., published in 1230; the Sext, added by Boniface VIII.; the Clementines, issued in 1318; and the Extravagants, or uncodified edicts, of the succeeding popes. A knowledge of these was the scientific equipment of the ecclesiastical jurist, but the texts were not authoritative. . . .

[1] *Ecclesiastical Courts Commission*, 1883, i. 24.

That **is** the exact point; **these** texts 'were not authoritative.' We eagerly turn **to the next** sentence, assured that **the proof or the illustration** is coming. 'The English **barons and** the king **at the Council** of **Merton** refused to **allow the** national **law of marriage to be modified by them** [*i.e.* by these papal texts], **and it was held that they were of no force at all when and where they were opposed to the laws of** England.' So no more need **be said of the canon law** of **Rome.**

It would seem, then, that, after all, we have been misunderstanding **our guide. He has been thinking of one** thing, **we** of **another; he of the extent of the field, we** of the **course of agriculture; he of the state, we of the church.**

For **what is the good old story?**[1] **In the twelfth century the church in England and elsewhere became definitely committed to the doctrine that a marriage between two persons might legitimate their already born children. This doctrine was unacceptable to the king's court. As a general rule, when in that court a question arose as to a person's legitimacy, it was submitted to the ecclesiastical judge for his decision. Owing to the divergent theories of the two courts, difficulties arose. The temporal justices, in order to protect their own rule, took to asking the bishops to answer in express words the narrow question whether a person was born before or after the marriage of his parents. Then at Merton the bishops, urged on by Grosseteste, said that they would not and could not answer this question, since so to do would be contrary to the common form of the church: in other words, by so doing they would be participating in the administration of a rule that was opposed to the church's teaching. Thereupon they**

---

[1] It is excellently told by Dr. Makower, *Const. Hist. of the Church of England*, pp. 422, 423.

asked the barons to change the English law of inheritance, and received the well-known reply. The baronial *Nolumus* was preceded by an episcopal *Nolumus et non possumus*. The result was that each party maintained its own ground. In a short while, however, the state discovered that in this instance it could do well enough without the bishops' help, and, instead of sending the objectionable question to them, sent it to a jury of lay folk. The honours were divided; but the state, as by this time its habit was, took the odd trick.

Here, then, we may see a collision between the claims of the church and the claims of the state; but there was no collision between the law of the church of England and the law of the church of Rome. Quite the contrary. The principle for which the English bishops struggled was part and parcel of the canon law of Rome. That they conceived it to be the law of the church merely because one supreme pontiff had decreed it and another had included it in his brand-new statute book I am not saying; still, as a matter of fact, the rule for which they contended was the rule laid down in a famous decretal.[1] Therefore this episode in the border warfare between church and state throws no ray of light on the nature of the law administered by the courts of the English church, except in so far as it shows that at one particular point the law of that church did not differ from the law of the church of Rome. Of course, if any one were to prove that after the day at Merton the courts Christian, when acting within the sphere in which they were free to act, rejected the theory of legitimation by subsequent marriage, then indeed proof would have been given of a case in which the Anglican swerved from the Roman canon law. Now there was a sphere within

---

[1] *Tanta est vis*, c. 6, X. 4. 17 : Alexander III. to the bishop of Exeter. Grosseteste cites this decretal in his letter to Raleigh (*Epistolae*, p. 78).

which the English church was at liberty to administer a law of legitimacy without coming into contact with the secular power. A man who was not legitimate could not be ordained without a dispensation. What did the English bishops in this case? It seems hardly doubtful that they continued to administer that canonical and, if we please so to call it, Roman rule which the English barons had refused. John of Ayton treats legitimation by subsequent marriage as an important practical matter.[1] He has a long discussion of a particular case. A clerk in minor orders marries the woman who has already borne him a son. Is that son legitimated, or are we to say that fornication, when committed by a clerk, is so grave a crime that the progeny of this *damnatus coitus* are not *naturales filii*, but mere *spurii*, who are incapable of legitimation? Such a question would have no meaning in England were it not that, despite all that happened at Merton, the English church within the province that is conceded to her is retaining a rule which, however dissonant it may be from the law of the English temporal courts, is in perfect harmony with the decretals. John of Ayton does not stand alone. John de Burgh more than once tells us how bastards are legitimated by the marriage of their parents.[2] Unless, then, these English canonists mislead us, the old ecclesiastical rule was enforced in England until the Reformation or some yet later time.[3] And here it may not be impertinent to ask whether the law which excluded bastards from orders has ever been definitely repealed, and whether our English bishops are actually enforcing it. If a

---

[1] Joh. de Athona, p. 38, gl. ad v. *contracta fuisse*.

[2] *Pupilla Oculi*, ed. 1510, ff. 76, 111 d.

[3] Late in the seventeenth century Godolphin, *Repertorium Canonicum* (ed. 1680), p. 487, wrote thus: 'If a man hath issue by a woman, and after marry the same woman, the issue by the common law is bastard, and *mulier* [i.e. legitimate] by the ecclesiastical law.'

negative answer must be given to both these questions, then I think that we have here a valuable hint as to some of the less obvious among the effects of the protestant Reformation. An old rule of catholic canon law was forgotten or ignored, though no one could have laid his finger on any text by which it was expressly abrogated.[1]

But, to return to the middle ages, this tale of 'special bastardy' I take to be a typical tale, illustrative of a common course of events. Of that debatable land which is neither very spiritual nor very temporal the state seizes a portion. The portion that it seizes it cultivates after its own fashion, with but little regard for the canon law of Rome, or for canon law of any sort or kind. The portion that is left to the church is cultivated by the church after its own fashion, with little, if any, regard for the secular law, but with great regard for—nay, in obedience to—the papal statute books.

Never in England, nor perhaps in any other country, did the state surrender to the ecclesiastical tribunals the whole of that illimitable tract which was demanded for them by the more reckless of their partisans. Everywhere we see strife and then compromise, and then strife again, and at latest after the end of the thirteenth century the state usually gets the better in every combat. The attempt to draw an unwavering line between 'spiritual' and 'temporal' affairs is hopeless. Such it will always be if so-called 'spiritual courts' are to exer-

---

[1] Ayliffe, *Parergon*, pp. 41, 208, still speaks as though bastardy were a disability. Blackstone, *Commentaries*, i. 459, says: 'But this doctrine seems now obsolete.' The modern text-books of ecclesiastical law seem to treat it as obsolete, but I cannot find that it has been repealed or judicially rejected. In recent times the document which described a bishop's confirmation stated that the elect had been found to be 'of a free condition, born in lawful wedlock, of due age, and an ordained priest.' See the report of *The Queen* v. *Archbishop of Canterbury*, State Trials, New Series, vi. 414.

cise any power within this world of time. So ragged, so unscientific was the frontier which at any given moment and in any given country divided the territory of secular from the territory of ecclesiastical law that ground could be lost and won by insensible degrees. In France, for example, under cover of some pretty fictions the clergy were slowly deprived of the *privilegium fori*, and the office of deciding whether a marriage was valid passed in fact, though not in theory, into the hands of the secular courts. We have only to consider the incurable vagueness of such phrases as 'testamentary causes' and 'matrimonial causes,' and we shall understand how easily one small annexation might follow another without any pitched battle, any shout of triumph or wail of defeat. The rulers of the church, therefore, had to tolerate much that they could not approve, or at any rate much that they could not approve in the name of the church. They could give and take without any sacrifice of first principles. No doubt there were principles for which they would have professed a willingness to die after the fashion of St. Thomas; but they were not called upon to shed their blood for every jot and tittle of a complex and insatiable jurisprudence. Popes, and popes who were no weaklings, had taught them by precept and example that when we are dealing with temporal power we may temporise.

If, therefore, we find, as we easily may, that the English secular courts are keeping to themselves certain matters which, according to a decretal, should be left to the spiritual courts, and if we find, as we easily may, that the English bishops are not persistently protesting against this usurpation, we must neither at once accuse them of a neglect of duty nor at once credit them with an Anglican canon law which differs from the Roman. The Roman catholic bishops in modern England have to 'tolerate' (is not that the correct phrase?) many legal arrangements that they cannot approve. They still, so I read, hold it to be the law of the church that clerks should not be sued in secular courts, and in this country no *concordat* has suspended this rule; but they make no endeavour to enforce it in all its generality.[1] If we either blamed them as careless shepherds or praised them for an incipient Anglicanism, I feel sure that in either case we should do them an injustice. *Dominus papa scit et tolerat.* But this is no new state of affairs. In every century from the twelfth onwards there has been a good deal of ecclesiastical law that has not been enforced. At times a good deal of temporal law has been in no better case, as witness certain English statutes about 'provisors.' The rudiments of the art of bargaining have long been familiar to church and state. More is demanded than is expected, and what is obtained is taken upon account.[2]

Were we to institute a comparison between the bargain struck in England and the bargains struck elsewhere, and to suppose this comparison to be made in the year 1300 or thereabouts, we should find that at two points the English church had been singularly successful. In the first place, the sentence of excommunication, when pronounced by the ecclesiastical courts, was enforced by the secular power with mechanical regularity and almost as a matter of course. The excommunicate was disabled from suing in the temporal courts: the

---

[1] Kirkpatrick, *The O'Keeffe Trial*, pp. 390, 397, 530. Cardinal Cullen: 'In countries where there is no concordat . . . the holy see has declared that breaches of ecclesiastical immunity are to be overlooked.' Mr. Purcell: 'Tolerated and winked at?' The Cardinal: 'Yes.'

[2] Some words of Innocent III. (c. 18, X. 3. 5), which Lyndwood (p. 208) quotes, put us at the right point of view: 'Quum multa per patientiam tolerentur, quae, si deducta fuerint in iudicium, exigente iustitia non debeant tolerari.'

contumacious excommunicate was thrown into gaol.¹ In the second place, the canonists had acquired what they hardly aspired to elsewhere, namely, an exclusive jurisdiction over testamentary causes and over the distribution of the goods of intestates. On the other hand, there were two points at which the English church had been singularly unsuccessful. The *privilegium fori* was confined within unusually narrow bounds, and secular justice kept a tight hold over all disputes that touched ecclesiastical patronage. About these two points a few words should be said. We are concerned to see whether there has been simply a struggle between church and state, or whether the church of England has been departing from the church of Rome and evolving a jurisprudence of her own.

The full extent of the immunity from secular justice that was claimed for the clergy was this: that no criminal charge was to be made and no 'personal' action brought against a clerk in any temporal court. We need not here discuss the exact meaning of the term 'personal' when used in this context. The contrast to it is 'real,' and the canonists admitted that actions in which the ownership of land was directly in debate, at all events if the land was not claimed by a church as free alms, were within the cognisance of the secular forum. It is unnecessary for us to attempt an exact delimitation of the personal from the real (Bishop Grosseteste found that this task was not easy), for in Edward I.'s day the king's justices had for some time past persistently traversed the assertion that in personal actions clerks enjoy the *privilegium fori*.² What had been conceded to them

---

¹ Hinschius, *Kirchenrecht*, v. 391 ff., for Germany; Viollet, *Bibl. d. l'École des chartes*, xxxi. 174 ff., for France.

² Grosseteste, *Epistolae*, 222, would allow the secular court to enter on a possessory action for land, e.g. the novel disseisin, against a clerical de-

was a 'benefit of clergy' in cases of felony. In our eyes this may seem a large, to the high churchmen of the thirteenth century it seemed an unduly small, concession. The list of felonies was brief, and if there was a charge of any minor offence, or if there was a civil action arising from contract or delict, the clerical defendant was to enjoy no privilege. In this respect the English differed markedly from the French settlement. In France nearly the whole of the ecclesiastical claim to a *privilegium fori* was allowed, though with admirable ingenuity the French lawyers of a later day practically withdrew what they nominally granted, and brought both the serious and the petty offences of the clergy within the range of the state's law.

The English settlement was the result of a severe struggle in the thirteenth century. To all seeming the high churchmen had on their side the letter of what might have been called a *concordat*, or at any rate the letter of the concession which Henry II. had been compelled to make after Becket's death.[1] Nevertheless we soon find that clerks are being sued in personal actions before the royal court, and Bracton tells us that this is being done every day.[2] Towards the middle of the century a storm that had long been brewing burst in vehement protest. A large party among the clergy complained that the church was deprived of her liberties. Grosseteste seems to have been their leader and spokesman. It is not unlikely that smouldering discontent had been fanned into flame by the appearance of Pope Gregory's book, just as a hundred years before a similar

fendant. The classification of such an action as 'real' is in harmony with English ideas. The 'reality' of the novel disseisin was one of the points disputed between Pierre de Cugnières and the bishop of Autun (*Biblioth. S Patrum*, Paris, 1589, vol. iv. col. 1211).

[1] Diceto, i. 410.
[2] Bracton, f. 401b: 'secundum quod videri poterit tota die.'

movement was stimulated by the Decretum.¹ At length a serious measure was taken; at least for a moment it looked serious. Archbishop Boniface and his suffragans uttered their mind in canons which were meant to be strong and in truth were noisy. They demanded the *privilegium fori* in all its amplitude. If a clerk was sued in a personal action before the bishop's court, the bishop was to refuse to appear before the king's judges and give an account of his doings, and the thunders of the church were to be dispensed in defence of his refusal.² But our bishops were reckoning without their pope. They sent their canons to him for confirmation. He thought this a very proper request, and urged the king to give way, but he would not confirm the canons.³ A few years afterwards Archbishop Peckham was in the sorry plight of not knowing whether these canons were or were not in force, since 'it was said' that an appeal to Rome had been made against them.⁴ Thenceforth the loudest of them were useless canons; the state ignored them, and Lyndwood could hardly bring himself to give them a gloss.⁵

Now we may see here a victory won by the state over the church. One of the main claims that have been put forward in the name of the church is repudi-

¹ *Ann. Burton.* 254, 362, 424; Mat. Par. *Chron. Maj.* vi. 357; Grosseteste, *Epist.* 214-220.

² Const. Bonifacii, Wilkins, *Concilia*, i. 747; Lyndwood, Appendix, p. 15.

³ *Foedera*, i. 424. For the king's appointment of proctors who are to urge his appeal against the constitutions, see Prynne, *Records*, ii. 983, 990.

⁴ Const. Jo. Peckham, Wilkins, *Concilia*, ii. 51; Lyndwood, Appendix, p. 26: 'Verbo vero recitato volumus concilium de Lambeth, quod . . . Bonifacius cum fratribus et coepiscopis suis temporis noscitur salubriter edidisse, ut circa ipsum, quod dicitur fuisse appellatione suspensum, qualiter procedi debeat videatur.'

⁵ Lyndwood, p. 92. The passage is quoted above, p. 56. Some bishops of Edward I's day were still maintaining the old claim; see Prynne, *Records*, iii. 367; but the battle had been decided.

ated by the state for good and all. It was none the less a victory because it was secured by the inaction of the pope at a critical moment, nor because that inaction may have been induced by means that were none too creditable. Neither Henry nor Urban are we defending. As to the English bishops, let us find some pity for them, some pity even for the blustering Boniface. They tried to do their duty, but were snubbed by their official superior. They tried to put in force 'the canon law of Rome,' or, as they would have said, the law of the universal church, and were taught that if there is a time for speech there is also a time for silence, and that zeal, even though it be a zeal for decretals, should be tempered by political discretion. Here, then, we have one eminent instance in which the canon law of Rome failed to obtain a home in England; but surely there is no reason why we should accuse our national church of being party or privy to the slight that was thus put upon the *ius papale*.[1]

The fight for the advowson had been lost and won at a much earlier time. While it lasted it must have been sharp. About half those texts in the Gregorian code that deal with the right of patronage are decretals sent in the twelfth century to English bishops, and the classical passage which tells how a cause which touches this right belongs exclusively to the ecclesiastical forum is a decretal addressed by Alexander III. to our Henry II.[2] But, in spite of Alexander and Becket, Henry established as English law the very opposite of

---

[1] Among the *Decisiones Dominorum de Rota* (ed. Aug. Taurin. 1579, p. 364) is a strong condemnation of the English 'custom,' which for many reasons is pronounced invalid. This decision is quoted by Hotman in the tract of his that is included among the *Traitez des droits et libertez de l'Eglise Gallicane*, 1651, p. 292. He argues that France, with all its Gallicanism, had allowed the clergy an immunity which England refused.

[2] c. 3. X. 2. 1.

this proposition.¹ In a short while our temporal courts had a whole scheme of remedies at the disposal of those who claimed advowsons or presentations, and **a writ** of prohibition **was** forbidding the courts Christian to meddle or make with this matter.² Anyone who has glanced at the plea rolls and the Year Books will know that a vast volume of litigation was thus diverted from the ecclesiastical forum, to the impoverishment of the canonists and the enrichment of the serjeants.

Neither Henry nor Becket can have been fully aware of the extreme importance of the question that was at stake, for they could not foresee the limitless claims over all ecclesiastical preferments that were to be made by the popes of a later age. Nevertheless there are some **who** will think that the **true** Magna **Carta of** the 'liberties of the English church' **is Henry's** assertion that advowsons are **utterly beyond the scope** of the spiritual tribunals. This **is the foundation of all** subsequent legislation against 'provisors.' The advowson is temporal property. '**Our** lord the king,' said the **parliament of Richard** II.,

and all his lieges are accustomed from of old and of right ought to sue in the court of our lord the king for the recovery of their presentations to churches, prebends, and other benefices of holy church, whereto they have right to present: the cognisance of plea of which presentations belongeth only to the court of our said lord the king by the ancient right of his crown, used and approved in all time by all his **progenitors,** kings of England.³

The advowson is temporal **property; the laws of the church and the courts of the church cannot touch it.**

¹ See Makower, *Const. Hist.* p. 435. As Henry did not admit that this was an **innovation, it** did not fall within the renunciation of Avranches.

² For **prohibitions** against dealing with advowsons, see Prynne, *Records, passim*; *Bracton's Note Book*, i. 187. A good example occurs in Prynne, *Records*, iii. 1066: the bishop of St. David's **claims an** exemption from the general law. See **also the case** of the bishop **of Tuam,** *ibid.* ii. 858.

³ Stat. 16 Ric. II. c. 5.

When the matter is thus stated, even the bishops of Richard II.'s day can, with certain reservations, publicly protest against the pope's behaviour. 'The crown of England' has been 'peaceably seised' from all time of the right to hold plea of advowsons. This immemorial seisin the holy father is disturbing. In so doing he is infringing, not the constitution of the catholic church, nor the rights of a provincial church (for of all this nothing is said), but the 'regality' of the English crown.[1]

To all seeming the maintenance of this principle by Henry II.'s successors aroused little opposition among the English clergy. They soon began to see that here lay their one bulwark against the invading army of Italians. They protest, but they protest in parentheses and half-hearted phrases. Grosseteste in the middle of his diatribe against the invaders of ecclesiastical liberties attacks a certain corollary that has been drawn from the main principle. The men of the court, he says, will argue that this corollary is fairly drawn: I am content for the moment to meet them on their own ground, and to dispute their minor rather than their major premiss; still I deny that laymen can be patrons of churches; I deny that secular judges can lawfully determine a suit about patronage.[2] Archbishop Boniface's council took up a similar position: *de facto* the king's court entertains suits touching the right of patronage; we will waive the question whether this is rightful or no, but now that court is going a little too far.[3] The zealous

---

[1] *Rolls of Parliament*, iii. 304.

[2] Grosseteste, *Epistolae*, p. 228: 'Sed dicunt curiales, Frustra iudicaret dominus rex de iure patronatus, nisi posset facere iudicii sui executionem. Ad quod respondendum est quod licet contra iustitiam habeantur laici ecclesiarum patroni, et iudices saeculares contra iustitiam determinent causas de iure patronatus; posito tamen quod haec fierent, ecclesia permittente sive dissimulante iudicium saeculare. . . .'

[3] Const. Bonifacii, Wilkins, *Concilia*, i. 748; Lyndwood, Appendix, p. 16: 'tunc intiment eis praelati praedicti quod non de iure patronatus, cuius

Peckham, we are told, was minded to reclaim the ground that was being lost. He desired, says a chronicler, to 'annul' the 'liberties' which the king had enjoyed from a remote time, but drew back in fear.¹ John of Ayton opposes law to practice: the king's court keeps to itself disputes relating to the advowsons of rectories, albeit this is contrary to the canonical laws.² So Lyndwood: as a matter of fact the king of England holds plea of the right of patronage, and says that this matter belongs to his forum, though according to the canon law the contrary is true, as we read in the decretal addressed to Henry II.³ The doctrine of our canonists seems to be that the church is, to use Grosseteste's phrase, 'permitting and dissimulating' this invasion of her rights. But there is no opposition of the law of the church of England to the law of the church of Rome. The king infringes the *ius canonicum*; he infringes the *leges canonicas*. In secret we may rejoice that he does so; but we must keep our joy to ourselves, unless, indeed, we say that long-continued usurpation has generated a prescriptive right.⁴

In modern days we wax very wroth with the bishop of Rome for his reservations, collations, and provisions;

cognitionem rex de facto exercet ... cognoscere intendunt.' See also *Ann. Burt.* p. 424.

¹ *Ann. Osn.* p. 285.

² Joh. de Athon, p. 96, gl. ad v. *collatio*: 'licet secus sit de cognitione huiusmodi secundum leges canonicas, Extra. *de iudi. quanto* [c. 3, X. 2. 1, Alexander to Henry II.].'

³ Lyndwood, p. 281, gl. ad v. *regia*: 'quantum de facto rex Angliae cognoscitur [*sic*] in causa iuris patronatus et dicit hanc causam ad forum suum pertinere, cum tamen contrarium sit verum de iure canonico, per ea quae leguntur et notantur, Extra *de iudi.* c. *quanto*.'

⁴ *Ibid.* p. 316, gl. ad v. *iure patronatus*: 'cuius cognitionem ad se pertinere vendicat curia regia licet causa iuris patronatus sit annexa spiritualibus et sic pertineat ad forum ecclesiasticum: *de iudi* c. *quanto*. Sed consuetudo dat cognitionem foro temporali, et hoc etiam valetur haec constitutio [Bonifacii archiepiscopi] in hoc loco.'

5

and no doubt we do well to be angry with him, for sometimes he was shamefully nepotic. But do we always apportion the blame with equity? The bishop of Rome lived at Rome or Avignon, or elsewhere beyond the high seas. In strictness we cannot accuse him of having done any act in England. His reservations, collations, and provisions did not execute themselves. For the more part they were executed by English prelates. But we must not be prodigal of hard words. By infinitesimally small degrees those prelates had been taught that all ecclesiastical benefices are at the disposal of the supreme pontiff. That many of the English clergy sincerely held this doctrine we can hardly doubt. Grosseteste had proclaimed it in the strongest words. *Scio, et veraciter scio domini papae et sanctae Romanae ecclesiae hanc esse potestatem, ut de omnibus beneficiis ecclesiasticis libere possit ordinare.*[1] Clement IV. could not improve upon this statement of the principle when in a notorious decretal he said, *Licet ecclesiarum, personatuum, dignitatum aliorumque beneficiorum ecclesiasticorum plenaria dispositio ad Romanum noscatur pontificem pertinere.*[2] The more we make of Grosseteste's heroism in withstanding Innocent IV., the worse we think of his logical position. And bad enough it was. He had conceded to the apostolic see a power of freely dealing out ecclesiastical benefices all the world over, and then had to contend that this power should be used, but not abused. Instead of the simple statement that the pope cannot lawfully provide clerks with English benefices, and has no more right to appoint a canon of Lincoln than the bishop of Lincoln has to appoint a patriarch of Antioch, we find this indefensible distinction between use and abuse, and are at once led on to discuss the demerits of the *nepotes*. How can such a discussion

---

[1] Grosseteste, *Epistolae*, p. 145.   [2] c. 2 in Sexto, 3. 4.

end? If the bishop disputes the 'idoneity' of a nephew, an appeal lies to the pope. The bishop who makes a stand against the pope at the line between use and abuse is indeed heroic; but his is the heroism of despair.[1]

Then the complaints of the commons led to some anti-ecclesiastical legislation. Perhaps when we are reading the statutes against 'provisors' we think too exclusively of the elective benefices, more particularly the bishoprics. They were, no doubt, an important matter, but of almost equal importance were the presentative and collative benefices. All the patronage that was in the hands of the clergy, in the hands of 'the men of holy church,' was subject to the control of the pope. He did not in principle scruple to interfere with the rights of lay patrons, but in practice he dealt much more freely with the rights of the bishops and abbots.[2] Every such interference was from of old a breach of English temporal law: that is to say, the papal 'provisor' would have had no defence to a *Quare impedit*. But the spiritual patrons did not dare or did not think it right to sue. That is the situation which is put before us in the famous petition of 1344. And now let us observe the remedy that is prayed for by the commons and accorded by the king, earls, barons, and justices. If a benefice, the patronage whereof belongs to any spiritual patron, falls vacant, and a 'provisor' appears upon the scene, the presentation is to lapse to the king or to other the

---

[1] Whether Grosseteste wrote the most famous of the letters attributed to him is not here the question. Without it there is quite enough evidence, as Jourdain admitted (*Excursions historiques*, p. 164), of his having withstood certain appointments thrust on him by papal legates.

[2] This seems clear in the *Calendars of Papal Registers*. Often the pope disposes of a named church, and then we cannot tell who the patron is. But very often he decrees that a certain man is to have 'a benefice' from some bishop or abbot. I cannot find that similar attacks are made upon the patronage held by laymen. Canonries were the staple commodity of the papal market, and these could be given without hurt to lay patrons.

lord of whom the advowson is immediately holden, albeit the patron is doing his best to present or collate. The laity say to the clergy: 'We cannot trust you in this matter; we must protect you against yourselves. If a papal provision is made to any of your benefices, and the provisor attempts to put it in force, you must forfeit for that occasion your right of presentation.'[1]

The statute of 1351 was not drawn in quite so offensive a form. It perhaps gives the spiritual patrons a chance of fighting the pope, 'if they dare and will'; but still it maintains a distinction between the lay and the spiritual patron.[2] There is no talk of a lay patron having to forfeit a presentation to which he is entitled as the owner of a parochial advowson. Laymen think that they are strong enough.[3] Also what is said of the elective benefices is remarkable. If the pope makes provision of a bishopric, the king is to collate: in other

---

[1] *Rolls of Parliament*, ii. 153: 'Pleise a nostre seignur le Roi establer qe si nul Ercevesqe, Evesqe, Abbé, Priour ou autre Patron espirituel des benefices, apres lavoidance des tieux benefices acceptez par provisours et occupez, ou par la Court de Rome reservez, ne presentent ou facent collation deinz les quatre mois, qe adonqes au Roi a cel foitz, si tiel patronage de lui soit tenuz, ou a autre de qi il soit tenuz, accresce action et title de presenter. Et tut soit il qe defaute ne soit trovez en tielx ... patrons espirituels, par tant qils presentent ou font collations deinz les quatre mois a tiels benefices, jadumeyns sils soient destourbez par provisions ou reservations de la Court de Rome, enqore nientcontresteant qils font ce qen eux est daver tieux presentementz ou collations, qe droit de presenter accresce au Roi, ou as autres, come desus est dit, a cel foitz.' The patron's right to present or collate on a subsequent avoidance is then saved.

[2] 25 Edw. III. stat. 4; *Statutes of the Realm*, p. 317. As the reader will see, if he studies the statute closely in the Commissioners' edition, a little difficulty is occasioned by an ambiguous *ou*.

[3] This is written advisedly. There is a clause which deals with another case. A layman (*A. B.*) is patron of a monastery; if a papal provision be made either to the abbacy of the house or to the rectory of a parochial church appropriated to that house, then *A. B.* will have six months wherein to present. Even in this case the lay patron has the usual six months. The case in which a layman owns the advowson of a parish church is not dealt with.

words, the chapter is to lose for that occasion its normal, if shadowy, right of election. An excuse for this disfranchisement is given. The theory is propounded that of old the kings used to collate to bishoprics, and that they only granted the right of election upon a condition that has been broken. Now legislation which deprives chapters of the right to elect, bishops of the right to collate, spiritual patrons of the right to present, seems to me to deserve the name that I have ventured to give to it: it is anti-ecclesiastical legislation. No wonder, then, that the English bishops carefully abstained from taking any public part in the enactment of this statute.[1]

The statute put too much power into the hands of a king who had always some object to gain by chaffering with the court of Rome. But no statute could have been thoroughly successful, for no statute could effect a radical change in the opinions that men held touching the constitution of the Christian church. In 1409 there came before the king's court a cause in which the king sought to oust Henry Chichele, then bishop of St. David's, and afterwards archbishop of Canterbury, from a prebend in the church of Salisbury which he was retaining by virtue of a papal dispensation. Seemingly by way of afterthought, the king's advocates had recourse to the statute of 1351. Chichele's counsel asserted that the statute had never yet been put in

---

[1] In the interesting case of *The King v. Chichele*, which is thrice reported in the Year Book of 11 Hen. IV., we have (f. 77) this statement: 'In cases where provisions were made upon bishops, abbots, or other patrons, they might well, by our law, sue a *quare impedit* or a *praemunire facias*, at their election, for the Statute of Provisors was not made because there was any lack of an action for the patrons, since they had an action by our law (which well proves that by the law of the land the pope cannot oust anyone from the right that is given to him by the law of the land in case he will sue for it), but the Statute of Provisors was made because the spiritual patrons were in some sort disturbed, and dared not, because of the pope, sue for their right in the king's court.'

force,[1] and we have good reason for believing that this statement, if exaggerated, was not very far from the truth. So, too, the Year Books seem to show that the *praemunire* statutes were rarely brought into court until the temporal lawyers discovered that they had here a new weapon which could be used against the English ecclesiastical tribunals. Whether this use of them was foreseen by their framers is a moot point; but the petition of 1344, which is the root of all the subsequent legislation, prayed that suits, in which the judgments of the king's court were called in question, might not be brought in the court of Rome 'or other court Christian'; and it is by no means improbable that the English ecclesiastical judges had pronounced the censures of the church upon laymen, or at any rate ecclesiastics, who availed themselves of the law of the land as a defence agaist papal provisors.[2] Be that as it may, such protection as English clergymen enjoyed against 'the sovereign patron of holy church'[3] was due to Henry II.'s

---

[1] Y. B. 11 Hen. IV. f. 38.

[2] *Rolls of Parliament*, ii. 152 : 'Por ce qe avant ces heures ne fut pas ordeignez certeyne penance ne punissement contre ceux qi pursuent en la court de Rome pur anientir et adnuller le juggementz renduz par dues processes en la court de roi sur presentementz des esglises ... ou autre quecunqe juggementz renduz illoeques ... par qoi prie la communaltee du roialme qe accordez soit et establi qe si nul mes face tiels seutes en la court de Rome ou autre court Cristiene ... eit perpetuele prisone ...' I find it hard to believe that so general a phrase as 'or other court Christian,' was introduced merely because the Curia Romana might be at Avignon or elsewhere. Then in stat. 27 Edw. III. c. 1, we have a punishment denounced against such as impeach the judgments of the king's court 'en autri court.' In stat. 16 Ric. II. c. 5, we have, 'en la courte de Rome ou aillours.' The complaints of the clergy Wilkins, *Concilia*, iii. 533, 555) against the misinterpretation of the statutes may have been well founded; but we cannot estimate their justice until the cases to which they referred are in print. If the English ecclesiastical courts were, e.g., excommunicating those who contested the validity of papal provisions, this case would fall within the spirit as well as within the letter of the statutes.

[3] So called by Chief Justice Thirning in Y. B. 11 Hen. IV. f. 78.

victory, to the numerous writs of prohibition which taught the ecclesiastical courts that they had nothing to do with advowsons, to the establishment of a principle which Grosseteste condemned, and which Lyndwood treated as contrary to the canon law. This becomes plain when we contrast England with other countries. At the Council of Constance, the Germans and the Romance nations were glad to obtain by temporary and precarious concordats far less than was secured from of old by the temporal law of England to all English patrons who had the courage to sue for their rights.[1]

The story of papal 'provisions,' however we may tell it, will always be dismal; but it will be an incredible tale of cowardice and imbecility if it has not for its background a widespread persuasion that, whatever may be said against this or that appointment, the general principle upon which the pope relies is warranted by the law of the church. Adam of Murimuth, chronicler and canonist, has told us that at Avignon Englishmen were reputed to be 'good asses'; he has told us that 'they suffered wise men gladly, seeing that they themselves were fools.'[2] Adam himself was one of the wise, for he had accepted a modest 'provision' at Hereford,[3] and yet, perhaps, one of the fools, for he had been the 'executor' of many a papal mandate. But such words as *fools* and *asses* are too feeble to describe the Englishmen, and more especially the English bishops, of the fourteenth century, if they regarded the pope's action as

---

[1] Hubler, *Die Constanzer Reformation* (Leipzig, 1876), pp. 78, 115. It became an article of the Gallican liberties that 'le juge royal connoist du possessoire des bénéfices.' See *Preuves des libertez*, p. 699. But in England, from century xii. onwards, the royal court claimed an exclusive cognisance as well of the *petitorium* (writ of right of advowson), as of the *possessorium* (darrein presentment, *quare impedit*, etc.)

[2] A. Murimuth, pp. 28, 175.

[3] *Calendar of Papal Registers*, ii. 123.

utterly wrongful and lawless. Mixed with much that was base and selfish, there was something that was yet more dangerous, because it was more honourable, a faith, a creed, a principle. Very unwilling were even the laity to admit that fault could be found with this creed. When an act of parliament suggests that the holy father cannot know what he is about, but is being deceived by the lies of avaricious suitors, there is less of intentional irony in this apology than we are quick to detect.[1] How deep-set was the belief in the pope's legal right to deal freely with ecclesiastical benefices and with the property of the churches we may learn from the querulous Gascoigne. He was fully convinced that most of the enormous mischiefs which he saw around him, and which in his view were rapidly ruining the church of England, were due to the action of the popes; that the popes were weak or wicked men; that the only excuse that could be urged for them was, that if for a moment they lapsed into wisdom and virtue they would be poisoned by their cardinals. His dissatisfaction was not the less unfeigned because the conscious merit of a certain chancellor of the university of Oxford had never met with a becoming reward. And yet the only two remedies that he can propose are a prayer that the popes may be brought to a better frame of mind, and a suggestion that, instead of abusing, they should now begin worthily to use their rights, as, for example, by a measure of disendowment, a transfer of property from the religious houses to the parish churches. It is the old hopeless tale. The powers that were given for edification are being employed for demolition; the sheep are flayed, not fed; nevertheless the powers were given, the flock was committed to the shepherd. Let us hope and pray that the *plenitudo potestatis* will some day be

[1] 38 Edw. III. stat. 2.

wielded, as once it was, for righteous ends.[1] Meanwhile there is nothing for it but impotent ejaculation: *Heu! Heu! O domine deus! O papa Romae! O Symon! Heu! Heu!* The story of papal 'provisions,' however we may tell it, must be dismal; but it need not be disgusting, and yet, unless we make it disgusting, we shall never make it compatible with the supposition that our ecclesiastical courts were freely criticising decretals and rejecting what was unsuited to English ideas.

At this point a few words of explanation may be necessary. When we contrast the action of the English church with that of the English state (and to do this we are compelled), we are not of necessity contrasting the behaviour of the clergy with the behaviour of the laity. Even at any one moment the clergy was a miscellaneous mass, and few generalities about its thoughts or its doings would be true. It is very possible that at times many or most of the clerks in England wished well in their heart of hearts to certain anti-ecclesiastical efforts of the temporal power, and rejoiced at the issue of prohibitions. But more than this can be said of that early age, the twelfth century, which drew the principal lines that were to separate the two jurisdictions. It was a time when the king's court was full of bishops and archdeacons, and we may well believe that it was with their right good will that the advowson was handed over to the temporal power, and thus withdrawn from the

[1] *Loci e Libro Veritatum*, pp. 147, 148, 150: 'Dominus enim papa dispensator est bonorum quae committuntur ecclesiae, unde ea in illos usus potest papa conferre et illis hominibus qui melius possunt, sciunt et volunt bona ecclesiae ad laudem Dei et ad animarum salutem melius expendere. . . . Dominus papa, Christi vicarius, potest terras et redditus qui dantur cacteris [certis?] locis et monasteriis alienare et conferre aliis locis et ecclesiis parochialibus. . . . Sic Christi vicarius, dominus papa, qui est dispensator et minister bonorum ecclesiae auctoritate Christi, potest in Dei cultum augmentandum et lucrum animarum, res datas in usus alicuius ecclesiae disponere et prudentiae alicuius viri in commendam tradere . . .'

sphere of ecclesiastical law, Roman influence, and begging letters that were almost 'provisions.' Some of these prelates were in all likelihood far more at home when they were hearing assizes as *iusticiarii domini regis* than when they were sitting as *iudices ordinarii*, and they were already leaving the canon law to their schooled officials. For a compromise which bartered the advowson against the testament, there was much to be said. Even at a later time, when ordained clerks had forsaken the bench, they still peopled the chancery. Those writs of prohibition against which the clergy protested in their assemblies must often have been drawn by ordained clerks, settled by 'masters' who were doctors of the canon law holding abundant prebends, and sealed with a seal whose custodian was a bishop. There never was wanting a supply of persons duly qualified and somewhat eager to serve the state and hold the benefices of the church. Many a medieval bishop must have wished that, besides having two capacities, he had been furnished with two souls, unless, indeed, the soul of one of his subordinates would serve as an *anima damnanda*. Parties and partisans there have always been. If Grosseteste was a clergyman, so also was Bracton; they held diametrically opposite opinions about the *privilegium fori*.[1] We, however, are concerned, not with classes, but with institutions. We must not attribute to the state the acts of this or that baron; we must not attribute to the church the opinions of this or that bishop. It is of the constitutions that were promulgated in ecclesiastical councils, and the rules that were enforced by ecclesiastical courts, that we

---

[1] This must be my apology, if any be needed, for carrying back the term *high church* into the middle ages. By a *high churchman* I mean one who presses the more extreme claims that are made in the name of the church against the secular power.

make our question. Laws, it may be remembered, are often obeyed and administered by those who have little love for the laws or the lawgiver, but are persuaded that he has the right, or at least the power, to bind and to loose.

And now, returning to our main theme, we must remark that when the state has appropriated any tract of the debatable land, it imposes its own law upon that tract. The king's justices, even when they were dealing with affairs which were, or had been, claimed by the canonists, did not profess to administer the law of the church. Had they made any such profession, they would have added insult to injury. They administered, in all cases that came before them, not the law of the church, but the law of the realm, and in so doing they paid little regard to canons and decretals. It must be allowed that during an age which extends from Henry II.'s to Edward I.'s reign, they were learning a good deal from the church's lawyers. A class of professional canonists is older than a class of men professionally expert in English temporal law, and the secular courts adopted many suggestions from without. Still here we have no more than the acceptance of hints, and after the middle of the thirteenth century the temporal lawyers were becoming deeply and confessedly ignorant of *la ley de seinte esglise*. It is true that they were in general willing to co-operate with the canonists in producing an harmonious result. The man who is legitimate enough to be ordained, but bastard enough to be excluded from an inheritance, is a rare example of those inelegant results of a conflict of laws which have usually been avoided. For all this, there are numerous instances in which we may be sure that the king's courts decided in one way a question which would have been decided in another could it have come before an ecclesiastical tribunal. John of Ayton mentions one which may serve as an example. An abbot borrows money, and gives a bond under the abbey's seal for its repayment. The canonist, before deciding that the abbey was bound, would be inclined to discuss the manner in which the borrowed money was expended. But the law of the realm is not so subtle; it has an archaic reverence for sealed parchment, and, says John, will hold the abbey bound, 'even though the money were thrown into the sea.'[1] The clerical defendant who was sued in a personal action before the secular court, would, at a hundred points, have found there a law different from that which would have awaited him had he enjoyed the *privilegium fori*. The two procedures, for one thing, were radically different. And so, when once the advowson had been securely captured by the royal court, it became the subject of temporal law. Already in Bracton's day a large mass of rules had grown up around it; about hardly any other subject does he cite so many precedents. This mass of rules was English temporal law. Very curious law some of it was, and very unlike anything that a canonist would have written *de iure patronatus*. That it was English temporal law I must repeat, for, so it seems to me, misleading phrases have been used in this context.

It is well known, and often it is boastfully said, that the law about the 'lapse' of presentations that was enforced in England differed in a good many details from the classical 'canon law of Rome.' In particular, while the one gives to the patron, be he hallowed or be he lay, a term of six months wherein to present his clerk, the other will have no equality between clergy and laity, but allows the clerical patron six and the lay patron but four months. Now this seems to be one of those cases

[1] Joh. de Athon. p. 150, gl. ad v. *quam ecclesiis*.

in which the king's justices desired to effect in a general way the laudable objects of the law ecclesiastical. Obviously it is undesirable that a church should be for any long time void of a pastor. So a law of 'lapse' or 'devolution' is wanted. How the divergence was caused, it would be difficult to say. The classical canon law about this matter is not to be found plainly stated upon the face of the Decretales Gregorii, but can only be obtained by a somewhat elaborate combination of texts. The third Lateran Council had allowed the patron no more than three months; but certain decretals were supposed to give the clerical patron six, while the layman's three were extended to four. The interpretation set upon these texts was confirmed by Boniface VIII. in the Sext.[1] But before the days of the Sext, the English justices seem to have established the rule which gives six months in every case. Whether they thought that they were adopting the law of the church in its entirety, or whether they deliberately overruled it in the interests of equality and lay patrons, is a very difficult question, which I must not take upon me to decide.[2] But in any case, the rule that they established was a

[1] See Hinschius, *Kirchenrecht*, iii. 46. The texts are cc. 3. 22. 27, X. 3. 38; c. 2, X. 3. 8; c. un. in Sexto, 3. 19. I have seen in a manuscript belonging to Caius College, Cambridge (No. 54), a treatise by an Italian lawyer who lived under Gregory IX., in which the question between four and six months is debated at length, and the solution that became orthodox is not even proposed. This treatise begins thus: 'Super accionibus communibus compositi sunt libelli per gratiam Iesu Christi.' I take it to be the work of Roffredus.

[2] *Bracton's Note Book*, pl. 205, 308, 438, 513, 883, 1389, 1570. These cases seem to show both a belief that the Concilium Lateranense is being enforced, and at the same time a practice of allowing six months in all cases. So Bracton, f. 241, Britton, ii. 176, Fleta, p. 321, speak as if the decree of the council always gave six months. It seems possible that our courts were misled by Con. Lat. III. 8 (c. 2, X. 3. 8), and overlooked Con. Lat. III. 17 (c. 3, X. 3. 38). Selden, *Hist. of Tithes*, ch. 12, § 5, could offer no more than 'a roving conjecture' about this matter.

rule of English temporal law, not a rule of English ecclesiastical law. The only ecclesiastical law about lapse that Lyndwood knew was the classical *ius commune* of the church, which gave the clergyman six and the layman four months.¹ He indulges in a discussion of the question how long the bishop must wait when the advowson is disputed between two would-be patrons, one of whom is, while the other is not, a layman. He is inclined to hold with some of his foreign doctors that in this case there will be no lapse until six months have expired. And this, he says, is the more probable opinion in England, where causes touching patronage belong to the royal forum.² This last remark seems to stamp as academic the whole of the preceding discussion. In England the king's court has grasped the advowson, and the practical law relating to it is English temporal law.³

There was perfect reciprocity. If the temporal courts were incompetent to administer *la ley de seinte esglise*, the spiritual courts were incompetent to administer *la ley de la terre*. The English temporal 'common law' and the statutes of the English kings set limits to the doings of the spiritual courts, but did not prescribe what those courts should do, nor the judgments that they should pronounce. We should hardly guess from

---

¹ Lyndwood, p. 215, gl. ad v. *devolvatur* : 'scilicet per lapsum sex mensium in patronatu clerici. Alias quatuor mensium ubi laicus est patronus. Extra. e.c. *cum propter* 'c. 27, X. 3. 38'.'

² *Ibid.* p. 216, gl. ad v. *neutri*.

³ In the version of the Provincial Constitutions, printed at the end of the Oxford edition of Lyndwood's book (p. 2), one of Langton's ordinances is made to end thus : ' Et licet de iure canonico clericus semestre, laicus vero quadrimestre tempus habeat praesentandi, tamen de statuto domini regis Angliae hodie uterque habet tempus semestre.' This (see Wilkins, *Concilia*, i. 586) seems to be no part of the constitution, but a lawyer's note, and we may well doubt whether there had been any royal statute touching this matter. But observe that the contrast is not between English and Roman canon law ; it is between the *ius canonicum* and a royal statute.

Lyndwood's book that secular England already had a good deal of written and enacted law. If by chance he mentions a statute, he will be careful not to pledge his professional reputation to its existence. *Statuta regia non sunt de mea facultate*, he seems to say.[1] He did, indeed, include among the provincial constitutions the document which we know as *Circumspecte agatis*; it was for him an important document, because it stated the king's opinion as to the whereabouts of the line which divides spiritual from temporal jurisdiction; but he expressly tells us that *textus iste non este authenticus*, and he must not be taken to have admitted that the king can legislate for the church, or give to his courts what of right belongs to the officialities.[2]

A good instance of his indifference to merely temporal arrangements we shall obtain if we ask him under what law heretics are being burnt in England. Were we to put that question to the modern historian, he would tell us that they were being burnt under the statute of 1401. Lyndwood's answer is very different. His answer is that death by burning is the punishment prescribed by a decretal contained in the Sext. Heresy was in his view a spiritual crime, and it was for the church, not for the state, to say what should be done

---

[1] Lyndwood, p. 241, gl. ad v. *clericus*: 'quare autem non fuit idem statutum quoad laicos, potest esse ratio: quia contra laicos in eadem materia emanavit statutum regium etiam poenale, editum (*ut audivi*) in parliamento Glocestriae, ubi etiam facta fuit haec constitutio 16 die Novembris a.d. 1368 (*al.* 1378).' The statute of which Lyndwood 'has heard' seems really to be 36 Edw. III. stat. 1, c. 8 (A.D. 1362).

[2] *Ibid.* p. 97, gl. ad v. *vel consuetas*. As a matter of fact, it seems that no 'authentic text' of *Circumspecte agatis* has descended to us; to satisfy this term we require a document bearing the king's seal or an officially preserved record. But I do not think that this is what Lyndwood means. He means that this royal declaration does not bind a spiritual court.

with heretics. If a lay prince would not execute the church's law concerning this crime, he was to be excommunicated. Here in England the secular power had of late made due provision for the fulfilment of its duty; but the law that sent the heretic to the flames was a decretal of Boniface VIII., not a statute of Henry IV.[1] This view of the case was by no means perverse. Henry's statute authorised the burning of those heretics, and those only, who, according to 'the canonical sanctions,' ought to be relinquished to the secular court. What were those canonical sanctions? They were the titles *de haereticis* in the three papal law-books. We should not gather from Lyndwood's pages that any such statute as that of 1401 had ever been issued. Of a later statute—namely, that of 1414—he does take notice. According to a constitution of Innocent IV., he says, the heretic's goods should be divided into three parts, one of which should be given to the secular power which executes the judgment, another to the city (*civitas*) in which the heretic is condemned, and a third to the judge; but nowadays in England, under a royal statute, all such goods are applied to the king's use.[2] Apparently he regards this as an infringement of the *ius canonicum*; but it would be graceless to squabble over the wretched chattels that the heretic has left behind him when we have secured the main matter, the incineration of his body 'according to the canonical sanctions.'

For more than three centuries past our spiritual courts have been required to administer, and have constantly administered, certain acts of parliament. We

---

[1] Lyndwood, p. 293, gl. ad v. *poenas in iure expressas*, referring to c. 18 in Sexto 5. 2, a decretal which declares how the pope wills that certain constitutions of Frederick II. shall be enforced.

[2] *Ibid.* p. 293, gl. ad v. *occupentur*.

too easily forget that this is the result, the not unimportant result, of the Reformation. Though much has been done for the history of the medieval church, we still may detect traces of Cawdry's case and 'the king's ecclesiastical law,' where we hardly thought to meet them. To Lyndwood, 'the king's ecclesiastical law' would have been a contradiction in terms. Kings and parliaments and secular justices had it in their power to narrow the province of the law ecclesiastical, and might hedge it round about with writs of prohibition which, as a matter of fact, the bishops and their officials would not transgress; but it was not for kings or parliaments or secular justices to make or to declare the law of the church, or to dictate the decisions of the church's courts.

We have been trying to clear away the irrelevant matter that has collected round an interesting question. What was the theory of the decretals that prevailed in the English courts Christian during the later middle ages? Were the decretals regarded as statute law, or did the English church exercise any right of accepting some and rejecting others? In modern books and judgments we may see an assertion, more or less emphatic, that this right was exercised, that 'the foreign canon law' was only applied in England when it had been sanctioned by English custom, or had met with the approbation of the rulers of the English church. We may find also the assertion or assumption that all this is proved and no longer dubitable. But when we look for the proof, it evades us. Such, at all events, has been my experience.

It is with many hopes that we turn to the learned Gibson. In the following passage he seems to approach our question, and yet to leave it unanswered. He has been speaking of the theory put forward by Henry VIII.

in the Act concerning Peter's Pence and Dispensations,[1] and then writes as follows:[2]—

> Here we have a plain declaration that foreign laws become part of the law of England by long use and custom. And as the church of England, in many cases both of voluntary and contentious jurisdiction, had no other rule by which to proceed, so in admitting and practising the rules which they found there they had no restraints upon them, save these two, that they were adapted to the constitution of this church, and so were *proper* rules, and were not contradicted by the law of the land, and so were *legal* rules. Which last was the condition of their being received and practised here, as well before the Reformation as since: witness the canon for the legitimation of children born before marriage, which was openly rejected as contrary to the laws of England; together with the reckoning of the six months lapse by weeks and the allowance of four months only to a lay patron, neither of which could obtain here against the contrary usages of reckoning by calendar months[3] and allowing the full six months to the laity as well as clergy.

Now at the present day we shall not set much store by any statement about the medieval law of the church of England made in the preamble of a statute in which King Henry already appears as that church's supreme head, even though the imperious document has the decency to allow that it is 'for many years' that the bishop of Rome, 'called the pope,' has abused and beguiled his majesty's subjects. As to the remainder of Dr. Gibson's argument, though it may not have flown

---

[1] Stat. 25 Hen. VIII. c. 21.
[2] Gibson, *Codex Iuris Ecclesiastici* (1713), vol. i. p. xxviii.
[3] This is a trifling detail; but is there any good warrant for the statement made in English books that the allowance of calendar months is an English peculiarity? Hinschius, *Kirchenrecht*, iii. 47: 'Die Frist wird kalendarmässig ohne Rucksicht auf die Zahl der Monatstage berechnet.' All that Coke proves in 6 *Reports*, 62, is that in Edward II.'s day a bishop of Lincoln adopted the lunar reckoning and got into a scrape by so doing. A similar case of Edward I.'s day may be found in Prynne, *Records*, i. 1220; on the other hand, in a case of Henry VII.'s reign (Keilwey, 88), the lunar reckoning was adopted.

wide of his mark, it assuredly flies wide **of ours.** The rule that **a bastard** cannot by the marriage of his parents be made capable **of** inheriting English land is simply a rule of English temporal law; it **is** a rule evolved and enforced by our **secular courts, and** with **it** our spiritual courts have absolutely nothing **to do. The** rule **about** the lapse of presentations is in some sense rather more ecclesiastical, for the bishops are required **to take notice of it** and **to obey it.** Nevertheless it **is a** rule enforced by our secular courts. **If the** bishops tried **to act upon** a different rule, **and, for** example, **behaved as though a lay patron** had **only four** months **wherein to present, they would soon find themselves defending actions in the Court of Common Pleas. If these instances are adduced merely for the purpose of showing that** certain rules of **the 'foreign' canon law were inoperative in England, well and good: that thesis is proved. But they are irrelevant to any inquiry touching the measure of authority or binding force that English ecclesiastical judges attributed to the decretals. Did they or did they not put in force only such papal ordinances as were supported by 'long use and custom'? Did they or did they not hold that the decretals were to be obeyed because they emanated from one who by divine right could legislate for the catholic church? We shall get no answer to these questions by studying the doings of the Court of Common Pleas, or by noting that in England, as elsewhere, the field conceded to ecclesiastical justice by secular power is not so wide as popes and canonists would wish it to be.**

The other instances to which an appeal is commonly made seem to me to be equally irrelevant. Thus it is remarked that tithe was not paid in England of certain things that were tithable by the general canon law, in

particular of coal and other minerals.¹ But here, again, what we see if we go back to the fourteenth century is that the ecclesiastical courts were doing their best to give the law of tithes as large a scope as possible, that the laity were complaining of these efforts, and that the secular justices were issuing prohibitions.² By means of these prohibitions the king's courts were acquiring the power to decide what matters were and what were not tithable, and of this power, when they had acquired it, they made an unstinted use.³ No, the instances that are to prove the existence of a national canon law must be instances of another kind. We must see an ecclesiastical judge, whose hands are free and who has no 'prohibition' to fear, rejecting a decretal because it infringes the law of the English church, or because that church has not 'received' it.⁴

[1] Hale, *History of the Common Law* (ed. 1820), p. 28: 'For there are divers canons made in ancient times and decretals of the popes, that never were admitted here in England, and particularly in relation to tithes, many things being by our laws privileged from tithes, which by the canon law are chargeable (as timber, ore, coal, etc.) without a special custom subjecting them thereunto.'

[2] This had begun as early as 1237 (*Ann. Burton.* p. 254).

[3] Selden, *History of Tythes*, c. 8, § 29-35. *Registrum Brevium Originalium*, f. 54 b: 'Nota que les justices dient que dismes ne serront donés forsque des choses que profitent d'an en an, et ceo per memorie [corr. manurance] de home, mes c'est encounter decretall. ... Et auxi de carbonibus nec de quarera et auters semblables, ils s'accordent en nul maner a consultation, pur ceo que parsons prent disme del blee que crest sur les carbons, per qui il ne prendra de eux.' Fitzherbert, *Nat. Brev.* f. 53; *Rolls of Parliament*, ii. 370, iii. 591.

[4] The longest list that I have met with of 'canons that were not received here' occurs in Stillingfleet's *Ecclesiastical Cases* (1698), p. 356. We have (1) the Merton story, (2) the story of the *bigami*, (3) investiture by the lay hand, (4) the *privilegium fori*, (5) the immunity of clerks from taxation, (6) laws against provisors, and (7) various points in the law of presentation to benefices. In none of these cases do we see an ecclesiastical court or council refusing of its own free will to enforce a decretal. If it were proved that in the later middle ages those courts held that there could be no marriage except 'in the presence of an ordained clergyman,' this indeed would be a case in point; but I cannot think that this is proved or probable.

In a certain polemical context it was perhaps legitimate, and if legitimate it was highly expedient, to ignore the difference between the acts of the state and the acts of a national church. The pope of the counter-reformation was pressing his claims. The reply to him was that never at any time—no, not in the golden age of faith and papacy—had his laws been integrally enforced among us. The national ranks were to present an unbroken front to the enemy; church and state were to stand, and were always to have stood, shoulder to shoulder. To France we must look if we would see this manœuvre dexterously executed. The illustrious lawyers who formulated the creed of Gallican liberties were as adroit as they were learned. Still for all their learning and all their adroitness there is a weak point in their case which is not to be concealed. The liberties for which they plead ought to be liberties of the Gallican church and not merely liberties of the French kingdom. They would like to say that the Gallican church (and let the word *church* be underlined) has never accepted the papal statute books, but has always maintained some tradition of an older and less Roman canon law.[1] From a very remote age they can produce satisfactory evidence, and again from a modern age there is testimony to be had; but as we cast our eyes over the famous catalogue of *preuves* we cannot help seeing that there is an intermediate period lying (to name its narrowest limits) between the date of the Decretum and the date of the

---

[1] But just at this point concessions had to be made. Leschassier, whose work is in the *Traitez des droits et libertez*, 1651, p. 444, says: 'Mais le decret de Gratian suivy des livres des decretales ayans esté leu en escoles instituees exprés, glosé, commenté, les hommes graduez en iceluy, et ces degrez pris pour capacitez aux benefices, et les saincts decrets alleguez aux sieges de iustice, selon qu'ils sont couchez en ce livre, l'impression venue apres luy, les escoles de Theologie et la doctrine scolastique instituee et dressee en quelques choses depuis luy et sur luy, on ne pense pas que iamais l'Eglise ait eu autre droit que cestuy là.'

schism, in which the chain, even when it has been strengthened by the spurious[1] 'Pragmatique' of St. Louis, is tenuous and brittle. Certain *preuves*, indeed, are still forthcoming; but are they proofs of the liberties of the Gallican church? They consist in the main of acts of a secular power which was controlling and curtailing the jurisdiction of the ecclesiastical courts, and was encroaching upon what the French prelates of that age held to be the liberties of the church in general and of the Gallican church in particular. Just as the compilers of Anglican liberties, when they tell the story of Merton, expect us to take the side of the barons, so the compilers of Gallican liberties, when they tell the story of Vincennes, expect us to take the side of Pierre de Cugnières. Now it may be true that the one real hope for a national church which should be wholly or mainly independent of Rome lay in the victory of the lay courts and the state-made laws at every point along the debated frontier line. But for obvious reasons this argument was not open to all controversialists, for it is apt to make the national church look like a spendthrift who must be 'interdicted' or forcibly confined to his house, lest he waste his patrimony and subject himself to the dominant will of some designing rogue. Unless, however, we have some such argument as this at the back of our minds, a glorification of the *appel comme d'abus* or our own writs of prohibition must seem a grotesque incident in a proof of the liberties of the Gallican or Anglican church. At any rate in the present day we, whose object is not to silence the papist, but to understand a certain tract of old history, are surely concerned to see whether such practical protest against the Roman theory as our ancestors were making

[1] Tardif, *Histoire des sources du droit canonique*, p. 276; Viollet, *Bibl. de l'École des chartes*, xxxi. 162; Esmein, *Histoire du droit français*, p. 639.

was being made in the name and by the organs of the church or in the name and by the organs of the state.

Just on the eve of the Reformation the doctrine that papal laws are not binding unless and until they have been 'received' becomes audible in the case of Dr. Standish. Once more that bird of evil omen, the criminal clergyman, was fluttering before the storm. Once more the blood of St. Thomas was liquefying. Henry VIII. had already invaded by a temporary and tentative statute the compromise which for some centuries past had settled the treatment of clerks accused of felony.[1] Clerks in minor orders, if accused of some of the very worst crimes, were no longer to enjoy the wonted immunity. This invasion was resented, and, as I read the story that is told by the anonymous law-reporter, some of the clergy, fired by the abbot of Winchcombe's sermon, were for reopening the whole of the old question. It was against the law of God, they said, that clerks should be 'convented' before the secular judges, though no one could deny that throughout the last three hundred years the indictment and arraignment of clerks in our courts of common law had been an extremely common event. In the debate that followed Friar Henry Standish argued the cause of the secular power, and asserted that the decrees which exempted clerks from lay justice had never been 'received' in England, and therefore were not binding. About the matter of fact he was in the right, for even in cases of felony our temporal courts had not allowed to the criminous clerk that full measure of immunity which the decretals claimed on his behalf. Then Standish was summoned before the convocation of the clergy to answer for his opinions. Among the erroneous doctrines charged against him was one which is stated in two ways:

[1] Stat. 4 Hen. VIII. c. 2.

Constitutio per papam et clerum ordinata non ligat regionem cuius contrario semper usa est:[1] *Iura positiva ecclesiastica non alios ligare quam recipientes.* He stood his ground; he repeated *quod iura ecclesiastica, quorum contrarium practicatum est per consuetudinem per 300 annos, non ligant nisi recipientes.* It seems clear that, though this may not have been the worst of his opinions, it was ill received by the assembled clergy. Then the king's justices began to talk of *praemunire*. Wolsey knelt before the king, protested that no attack on royal rights was intended, but protested also that the practice of bringing clerks before the temporal forum was contrary to the law of God and the liberties of holy church. He begged that the matter might be laid before the pope and his council in the court of Rome. Henry would not yield; he threw back in the face of the clergy the charge that they themselves were always transgressing the *decreta*. Now we must not manufacture arguments out of a story which is told by a nameless reporter, and which at a few points does not fit in very well with some other evidence. Also it should be noted that part of the high-church contention was that the immunity of criminal ecclesiastics was secured to them, not merely by the *ius positivum ecclesiasticum*, but also by the imprescriptible *ius divinum*, which contained that apposite text, *Nolite tangere Christos meos*. And by the way we must notice that very recently Pope Leo in the fifth Lateran Council had declared that according to the law of God as well as human law, laymen have no power over ecclesiastics, so that Wolsey's was an appeal to a foregone judgment, and indeed it is likely enough that the English clergy's renewed and belated demand for the *privilegium fori* was the outcome of this papal

---

[1] In the report this statement takes an interrogative form. Standish was asked *an constitutio . . . ligat regionem*, etc.

manifesto newly brought from Rome by the abbot of
Winchcombe.¹ But still Dr. Standish's assertion that
the *ius positivum* was not binding in a country which
had not 'received' it seems to have met, to say the
least, with little approbation among those who, if our
current theory be true, maintained it as a primary rule
in their ecclesiastical courts. 'What shoulde one poor
frier doe alone against all the bishops and the clergie of
England?' exclaimed the doctor. No doubt, as men
will in such cases, he was exaggerating his isolation, but
certainly he defended himself very ill if he had only
been repeating a commonplace of the English canonists.
Time, however, was on his side; his doctrine was soon
to become a commonplace, a statutory commonplace, of
the ecclesiastical courts.²

The proof of which we are in search must be found,
if anywhere, before the breach with Rome. To rely
upon testimony which comes from a later date would be
to beg the whole question. At this point in the argument we must become painfully aware that the problem of
legal history with which we have been busying ourselves
will, at least in some eyes, become merged in a much

---

¹ Bull of 5 May 1514: *Lateranense Concilium Novissimum*, Rome, 1521,
f. 133; Labbe et Cossart, xiv. 228; Hefele-Hergenrother, *Conciliengeschichte*, viii. 610. On 4 Feb. 1512 the abbot of Winchcombe (Richard
Kidderminster) was commissioned to attend the council as one of the
English representatives (*Letters and Papers, Hen. VIII*, 1509-14, pp. 320,
341). For more of him see Wood, *Athenae* (ed. Bliss), i. 62. I have not
seen positive proof that he was present at the council.

² For this story see Keilwey's *Reports*, ed. 1688, f. 180b; also *Letters
and Papers, Henry VIII*, 1515-18, pp. 351-54, and Mr. Brewer's *Introduction*, p. ccxxii ff. Almost at the same moment the bishop of London was
saying that his chancellor, Dr. Horsey, who was accused of murdering Hun
in the Lollards' Tower, could not obtain a fair trial, 'for assured am I if my
Chauncellor be tryed by any xii. men in London, they be so malicously set
in fauorem hereticae prauitatis that they wyll cast and condempne any clerke,
though he were as innocent as Abell'; Hall's *Chronicle*, ed. 1809, p. 579;
Letters and Papers, 1515-18, p. 1.

wider problem, or rather, it is to be feared, in a general controversy over the continuity and discontinuity of English ecclesiastical affairs. Let us, as far as may be, stick to our legal last. Our question must be whether one particular strand is continuous. Are we entitled to suppose that the treatment which 'the foreign canon law' received in our courts Christian before England had renounced the authority of the Roman bishop was substantially the same as the treatment that the aforesaid law received in those courts after that event? I cannot believe that this or anything like this is true.

The few words that will here be said about the effect of the Reformation will not be taken as an argument to prove that, had it not been for the absolute rejection of the papal primacy, our ecclesiastical courts would never have come by a theory which made the validity of decretals depend upon their 'reception.' The development of Gallicanism would be a sufficient warning against any such assertion, though, if we were to speculate about what might have happened, and were to compare England with France, we should have to remember once more that the one great work of an English canonist of the fifteenth century shows no liberal tendencies, no interest in the conciliar movement, nothing but a conservative curialism. However, with what might have been we have not to deal; we must speak of what happened, and the danger of any inferences drawn from the courts of the reformed to those of the unreformed church will be manifest.

In the first place, we have come upon what must be called a sudden catastrophe in the history of the spiritual courts. Henceforth they are expected to enforce, and without complaint they do enforce, statutes of the temporal legislature, acts of the English parliament. Henceforth not only is their sphere of action limited by the secular power—that is a very old phenomenon—but their decisions are dictated to them by **acts of** parliament —and that is a **very** new phenomenon. To take but **one** example, from 1540 onwards the marriage **law that they administer is in great** measure **law** dictated by **an act of parliament which has at one stroke** and **with many opprobrious words** consigned **to oblivion vast masses of intricate** old **canon law relating to** consanguinity **and affinity.**[1]

In the second place, these acts of parliament which the ecclesiastical courts must now administer are imposing upon them not merely new law but a theory about the old law, and it is in substance just that theory the truth of which is here in question. Henceforth a statutory orthodoxy will compel all judges to say that it was only 'by their own consent' that the people of this realm ever paid any regard to decretals or other laws proceeding from any 'foreign prince, potentate, or prelate.'[2] What is more, these same statutes will eloquently inculcate a free criticism of the old law—nay, a contempt for and a righteous indignation against certain portions of it. The bishop of Rome (called the pope) has during some indefinitely lengthy age been 'abusing and beguiling,' 'intangling and troubling' the king's lieges 'by making unlawful what by God's word is lawful both in marriages

[1] Stat. 32 Hen. VIII. c. 38. A few medieval statutes perhaps crossed the line, e.g. by (i.) fixing probate fees, (ii.) directing that a defendant in the ecclesiastical court should receive a copy of the libel, so that he might sue for a prohibition, (iii.) endeavouring by more or less indirect means to secure the institution of vicarages, and (iv.) bidding the bishops take measures for the punishment of clerical offenders. But the exceptions are of the rule-proving order. In the first case the ecclesiastical claim could be based on no higher title than 'custom.' In the second the secular power was protecting its own jurisdiction. In the third the state could fairly assert a right to dictate the terms upon which a licence to 'appropriate' should issue from the chancery. In the fourth the state dared not go beyond admonition and vague threats.

[2] Stat. 25 Hen. VIII. c. 21.

and other things.' And now the king, who 'is otherwise by learning taught than his predecessors in times past of long time have been,'[1] has discovered the fraud, and is going to annul and extirp much that has passed for law. Ecclesiastical judges who are expected to put in force these statutes will, without doubt, be 'otherwise by learning taught than their predecessors in times past of long time have been.' Some of these ecclesiastical judges will be laymen, who would have been incapable of sitting on the judgment seat to declare the law of the church, were it not for a statute which has swept away divers constitutions of the bishop of Rome and 'his adherents' the bishops of England, and at the same time has proclaimed that 'by the word of God' the king has and has always had full power and authority to exercise ecclesiastical jurisdiction.[2] It seems to me, therefore, that if we suppose that in the reign of Henry VIII. a new doctrine about the decretals began to prevail in the spiritual courts of this country, we are not supposing a change for which no adequate cause can be assigned.

But the great breach of continuity has yet to be noted. The academic study of the canon law was prohibited. No step that Henry took was more momentous. He cut the very life thread of the old learning. The ecclesiastical judges in time to come might administer such of the ancient rules as were not contrariant nor repugnant to the laws (newly interpreted) of God and

[1] Stat. 32 Hen. VIII. c. 38.
[2] Stat. 37 Hen. VIII. c. 17: 'Nevertheless the bishop of Rome *and his adherents*, minding utterly as much as in *them* lay to abolish, obscure, and delete such power given by God to the princes of the earth, whereby *they* might gather and get to *themselves* the government and rule of the world, have in *their* councils and *synods provincial* made . . . divers ordinances and constitutions . . . lest *their* false and usurped power, which *they* pretended and went about to have in Christ's church, should decay, wax vile, and be of no reputation, as by the said councils and *constitutions provincial* appeareth.'

the statutes of our lord the king; but they would not have been, like their predecessors in time past, steeped and soaked for many a year in the papal law-books and their ultra-papal glosses. And, as if this were not enough, Henry encouraged and endowed the study of 'the civil law,' and the unhallowed civilian usurped the place of the canonist on the bench. The significance of this change is sometimes overlooked. Owing to the rapid development of our own English system of temporal law, the civilian who was only a civilian had never found much to do in this country, and 'the civil law' seems to have been chiefly studied as a preparation for the canonist's more lucrative science.[1] The consequence is that we in England are apt to lump the legists and decretists together, and contrast them with 'the common lawyers.' Thus we are in danger of forgetting that in other parts of the world the legists and decretists had not always dwelt together in unity, and that just about those questions which were coming to the front in Henry VIII.'s day there was like to be open war between them. The rulers of the church had long known this: had long known that the jurisprudence of Justinian's books, if it was a useful handmaid, would be a terrible mistress. What else should it be? The first lesson that we learn if we open the Code is the very lesson that Henry was teaching, namely, that an emperor can legislate *De episcopis et clericis*, *De sacrosanctis ecclesiis*, nay, for the matter of that, *De summa trinitate et fide catholica*. What does the first chapter of the first title of the first book teach us? That the emperor fixed the faith of his subjects by reference to the standard orthodoxy of the

---

[1] In the England of the fourteenth century the unordained civilian was not unknown. Murimuth (pp. 171, 229) describes John of Shoreditch as 'doctor legum, advocatus et miles de consilio regis existens,' 'miles sapiens et iuris professor.' Also there were even among the bishops men who were *doctores legum*, and not to all seeming *doctores utriusque iuris*.

bishops of Rome and Alexandria. What an emperor did, a king who had 'the dignity and royal estate of an imperial crown' could undo. The theory of church and state which the civilian found in his books was the imperial papalism, the *Cäsaro-Papismus*, of Byzantium, and now what had been the one known antidote to this theory was to be placed out of reach: the schools of canon law were closed. If Henry was minded to be 'the pope, the whole pope, and something more than pope,'[1] he might trust the civilians to place the triple and every other crown upon his head. In the eyes of 'the common lawyers,' whose traditions were medieval, the church might still have appeared as a power co-ordinate with the state, a power with which the state could treat, co-operate, quarrel; but the civilian, whose sacred texts were shaking off the dust of the middle ages, would, if he were true to his Code and Novels, find his ideal realised when, and only when, the church had become a department of the state. The most superbly Erastian of all Henry's grandiose preambles (we might call it the *Unam sanctam* of the royal supremacy) introduces a statute that benefits the doctors of the civil law. They would not be ungrateful.[2]

Of the English civilians of the sixteenth century too little has yet been written; but we may know something of the doctrines that were being taught in the Oxford law-school about the year 1600 by the able and erudite occupant of the chair that Henry had founded. From Professor Alberico Gentili the young men who were preparing themselves for practice in our spiritual courts might learn a great deal about the old canon law (for

---

[1] Stubbs, *Seventeen Lectures*, 1886, p. 262.
[2] It is not an accident that the Protector Somerset desires 'a civil law college' in Cambridge; it is not an accident that his project is resisted by Stephen Gardiner.

the professor had read it under good masters), but they might also learn to loathe and despise it as a mass of bad Latin and brutal ignorance, the product of dark ages, in which the sacerdotal lust for power had filched from the kings and princes of the earth their God-given rights. They might learn also that it was the work of antichrist, and would be sent for their theology to Luther and Melanchthon, to Beza and Calvin. Perhaps, though Dr. Gentili called himself a loyal son of the English church, his inmost thoughts about religion were not exactly expressed by his words. In any case, however, he hated the canon law as the thoroughbred civilian should hate it; the days of servitude were past, and the time for revenge had come. Anything that Coke or Prynne may say in disparagement of the church's justice will seem tame or clumsy if we set it beside the fiery words of this legist, who is training the future expounders of English ecclesiastical law. With strict truth we may say that his words are fiery: *Flammis, flammis libros spurcissimos barbarorum, non solum impiisimos antichristi! Flammis omnes, flammis!*[1]

Professor Gentili would be no fair type of the English civilians of his time. They would not share in any full measure either his feud against, or his knowledge of, the old law of the church. They were no refugees: they were easy Englishmen, and year by year they were becoming more English and less cosmopolitan. So

---

[1] Gentili was a prolific writer; see Professor Holland's life of him in the *Dict. of Nat. Biogr.*, and is known to me chiefly through his *De Nuptiis* ed. 2, Hanover, 1614. The words quoted above come from lib. i, cap. 19. Throughout the chapter he rails at the canon law. I should suppose, from the numerous books cited by him in this and his other works, that he had read a great deal of what had been written by the Catholic canonists of all ages. Dr. Holland says that he did not escape the charge of being *Italus atheus*. I have seen nothing that would bear out an accusation of 'free thinking,' unless this lurks in his well merited laudation of heathen at the expense of Christian jurists.

large a use had been made of the king's supremacy, so acquisitive were the king's justices, that before the end of the seventeenth century a great part of the operative law which the civilians had to learn and administer was to be found in modern acts of parliament and judgments delivered by the secular courts.[1] Our civilians were fast acquiring what we may call the common law mind. If any peculiar mental attributes are to be ascribed to them, we may perhaps see some traditional bent towards monarchy. Gentili's Cambridge colleague was Dr. Cowell of the *Interpreter*. Also we may see a certain tendency to regard as open some questions that are very grave, questions about the dissolubility of marriage and the like.[2] Papacy was gone, and who could tell how much it had taken with it? The theory that the pope had never exercised lawful power within this realm was pressed to its uttermost.[3] A few words spoken by a judge in a court of common law were enough to abolish an old canon as unreceived, though the evidence of receipt was overwhelming.[4] All touch with continental thought was being lost. The popes and councils were mixed up in wondrous wise.[5] The glory had departed,

---

[1] See Godolphin's *Repertorium*, under such titles as 'Pluralities,' 'Non-Residence,' 'Tithes,' etc.

[2] Godolphin, *op. cit.* p. 501; see also Ayliffe, *Parergon*, p. 49.

[3] The high-water mark may perhaps be seen in the Irish *Case of Commendam* (Davis's *Reports*, p. 68).

[4] In Charles I.'s day Mr. Justice Doderidge declares that the rule *Filius patri non potest in ecclesia succedere* does not hold in the church of England: 'et issint, come Doderidge dit, fuit l'opinion d'un erudit civil lawyer' (Stoke v. Sykes, Latch's *Reports*, p. 191). In this case we happen to have singularly full proof that the rule was part of the English ecclesiastical law of the fourteenth century. Ayliffe, *Parergon*, p. 41, says that it is not 'safe' for a bishop to refuse a presentee on this ground, but that the archbishop usually grants a dispensation. See Phillimore, *Eccles. Law*, ed. 2, i. 312.

[5] Godolphin, *op. cit.* Appendix, p. 2: 'The third part of the body of the canon law was collected at the command of Boniface VIII., which contains these books: (1. *Sexti Decretalium*; (2) *Clementinarum*; (3) *Extravagantes*

and much of the profit too. Diplomacy had escaped from the civilian's clutch. The court of chancery was beginning to steal what even the old courts had spared. Thomas Fuller, in a happy phrase, tells us that 'although the civilians kept canon law *in commendam* with their own profession, yet both twisted together are scarce strong enough (especially in our own sad days) to draw unto them a liberal livelihood.'[1] It is not generally believed that the commendator gives much thought to the commended benefice. With the glory and the profit went the learning. That truly learned 'History of Tithes' was written by one who was proud to call himself 'a common lawyer.'[2] Lyndwood's text-book was thought to contain about as much canon law as a man need know. In the eighteenth century there was somewhat of a renascence, though it was left for a divine to compile a *Codex Iuris Ecclesiastici*. However, at this juncture the British fleet came to the civilian's rescue; it brought in 'prizes' for condemnation, and he enjoyed a short St. Martin's summer. A public international law that was intensely, if privately, national, was his chief contribution to the jurisprudence of the world; for the jurisprudence of the church he did and could do but little.

One word more, since we have been led to speak of schools and education. There seems to be sufficient proof that during the middle ages the schools of canon law at Oxford and Cambridge were singularly unpro-

---

Joh. XXII. et Communes.' Ibid. p. 358. After reading what Innocent III. did in 1209, we read how 'in the second Lateran Council, holden an. 1130,' a decree was made 'by the said Innocent III.' On p. 618 the fifth Lateran Council is put far out of its true place.

[1] Fuller, *History of the University of Cambridge*, sec. 6 ad fin.

[2] Selden, Preface. 'What hath a common lawyer to do, so they murmur, with writing of tythes. For by that name it pleases them to stile me, and I must confess I have long laboured to make myself worthy of it.'

ductive of anything that could be called original work. When we have mentioned John of Ayton, John de Burgh, and William Lyndwood, we have to all appearance mentioned almost the only English canonists who after the earliest years of the thirteenth century wrote books that met with any success. There may yet be in manuscript some surprises for us, and certainly the time has come when they should be diligently sought; but for the present we are compelled to speak of our English schools as singularly unproductive. Then, again, there seems to be in our libraries, in old catalogues, in medieval wills, and in university statutes, sufficient proof that our budding canonists were, as I have said, steeped and soaked for many a year in foreign literature, in the Decretum and the Decretals, in the works of Hostiensis and the Archdeacon, of William Durant and Johannes Andreae. Schools which produced so little that was English and absorbed so much that was foreign were not likely to be the nurseries of men who as advocates and judges would freely criticise, dispute, and deny the first principles of the science that they had laboriously acquired. This and no less is what we demand of them if we would see them handling the three papal law-books as mere 'manuals,' and not as 'codes of statutes.' In the Decretum they had been industriously taught that papal edicts stand on a level with the canons of the ecumenical councils, and then come three papal edicts, *Rex Pacificus*, *Sacrosanctae*, and *Quoniam nulla*, dragging statute-books in their train. We know that Reginald Pecock (who, however, did not escape prosecution for heresy) had his doubts about the donation of Constantine; but it is hardly to be supposed, I fear, that in English universities the lecturers on the Decretum interjected sceptical comments, or said that one canon was forged and another fudged. If such lectures were delivered, no pains should be spared in the collection of any traces of them that may yet be extant, for at present we have all too little to serve as a counterpoise for John of Ayton's reluctant and Lyndwood's exuberant papalism.

III. WILLIAM OF DROGHEDA AND THE UNIVERSAL ORDINARY

Let us change our point of view. The medieval church was a state. Convenience may forbid us to call it a state very often, but we ought to do so from time to time, for we could frame no acceptable definition of a state which would not comprehend the church. What has it not that a state should have? It has laws, lawgivers, law courts, lawyers. It uses physical force to compel men to obey its laws. It keeps prisons. In the thirteenth century, though with squeamish phrases, it pronounces sentence of death. It is no voluntary society. If people are not born into it, they are baptized into it when they cannot help themselves. If they attempt to leave it, they are guilty of the *crimen laesae maiestatis*, and are likely to be burnt. It is supported by involuntary contributions, by tithe and tax. That men believe it to have a supernatural origin does not alter the case. Kings have reigned by divine right, and republics have been founded in the name of God-given liberty.

When the medieval church is regarded as a political organism, as a state, it becomes very interesting. As a whole the constitution of this state may be unique, but there is hardly a feature in it for which we may not find analogies elsewhere. At various points it becomes a model for the constitutions of other and secular states, while itself reproduces many traits of the ancient Roman empire. Also the canonists, since they have had Justinian's books before them, have been fostering this resemblance, and applying to the pope whatever has been said of the *princeps*.

But the question which will be always in the minds of students of constitutions when they read ecclesiastical history will be the question whether there is to be federalism. The vast extent of the territory that was to be governed, and its division among divers races, each of which had an ecclesiastical history of its own, might lead us to expect that the church would in course of time make itself a model for federal states. No doubt, again, if we look back to remote days and still use the language of politics, we may see what can fairly be called the federation of churches, the federation of bishoprics under metropolitans, of provinces under a primate. An ideal which might under favourable conditions have become that of a definite federalism is never wholly absent: it comes to the front again and again. But when the Hildebrandine age has opened, and the church is in truth becoming a state, the dominant note is not that compromise between unity and plurality which is the note of federalism, but absolute and seamless unity. Nor is this wonderful. External warfare has a consolidating effect on internal structure. The church state had begun its prolonged struggle for jurisdiction with the secular states. Those coveted 'liberties,' that coveted independence, which could not be won from the temporal power by isolated, by allied, by federated churches, might be won by the church universal, indivisible, and monarchical. The illustrious forger knew it. The Pseudo-Isidore, so we are now taught, had no great wish to aggrandise the pope. That at least was not his primary object. He forges in the interest of Frankish bishops; but the 'freedom' of the bishops can only be secured by the genuine or spurious edicts of St. Peter's successors.

A single illustration of the close connexion between the two tendencies will be enough. Few legal texts have ever been more famous than the *Si quis suadente* of the second Lateran Council.[1] If anyone at the instigation of the devil lays violent hands upon a clerk or monk, he is excommunicate. He does not need excommunication; he is excommunicate, and, except at the hour of death, none but the pope can absolve him. Such a canon as this will be popular among the clergy, and its popularity will increase as the distance from Rome increases and the penitent's journey lengthens. And yet this is a dangerous canon if the churches are to enjoy even a moderate measure of home rule. The central power has an exclusive jurisdiction over a common offence, wherever it be committed, and every clergyman feels that his life and limb are protected, not by his bishop, but by the pope.

Even if there had been a vigorous sentiment making for federalism, the task of constructing the requisite machinery would have been difficult. There was no handy precedent for a federal state. There was a precedent both handy and imposing for an universal and an absolutely unified monarchy. Federalism, again, with its careful contrivances seems to imply a kind of far-sighted forbearance which was foreign to the middle ages. Also, if we treat the bishoprics as the federating units, the interposition of metropolitans, and in some cases of primates, between these federating units and the federal government would complicate the arrangement. Many other difficulties will occur to the mind of anyone who studies ecclesiastical affairs from the publicist's point of view. For example, if the popes are

---

[1] Concil. Later. II. c. 15 (Mansi, xxi. 530); c. 29, C. 17, qu. 4.

allowed to exempt certain religious houses and then whole orders from the power of the diocesan bishops, we shall have upon our hands classes of men who are members of the federal church, but are hardly for any purpose members of any of the federated churches.

But I would here ask attention to one particular feature in the constitution—namely, to the form which the judicial machinery of the church was assuming in that critical age the twelfth century. Judicial machinery is always important. It was, however, more important in the middle ages than it is now, for the function of declaring law was scarcely to be distinguished from that of making law. But even if we leave out of account the possibility that a power to declare law will become a power of open legislation, still judicial machinery will be important. If, then, for the moment we suppose ourselves to be champions of 'state rights,' or, in other words, of the rights which the federated units have against the federal whole, we must regard with serious anxiety the appellate jurisdiction of the court of Rome. What we shall look for and what we shall not find is any formula, or even any well-directed effort to construct a formula for the delimitation of those causes which, since some federal interest is involved in them, ought to come before a federal court. The *curia Romana* is not a federal court; it is an omnicompetent court of appeal. But this is not all. The so-called appellate jurisdiction which is being claimed and exercised is monstrous to the modern eye. It is not content with rectifying erroneous judgments; it (if we may so speak) anticipates presumably erroneous judgments and thence passes on to entertain all manner of complaints which a 'subject' may have to make of oppressive acts that have been committed or are being meditated by his 'prelate.' From this practice it was but a short step to the doctrine that the apostolic see is an omnicompetent court of first instance for the whole of Christendom, and this step seemed to be sanctioned by ancient and incontrovertible authority.[1] The jurist could state the matter thus: Normally the competent judge is the judge ordinary of the defendant's domicile; but Rome is the common fatherland of all men, as we learn from the Digest, and the pope is the judge ordinary of all men, as we learn from the Decretum.[2] Now, if any such principle as this can be made good in practice and on a large scale, then any talk of federalism, or of any idea at all similar to that of federalism, will be out of place. For a moment we might suppose that this doctrine, even if it commanded a theoretical assent, would encounter so many obstacles in the world of fact that it would do little harm and little good. In days when no steam engines rushed under the Alps surely the diocesan courts in England had no need to fear the competition of the court of Rome. But we are underrating the resources of the central power. It can delegate jurisdiction. Not only can it delegate jurisdiction in a general way, it can delegate jurisdiction over a particular cause. Thus, though it is true that the plaintiff must send a messenger to Italy for a papal

---

[1] c. 17, C. 9, qu. 3: 'Cuncta per mundum novit ecclesia quod sacrosancta Romana ecclesia fas de omnibus habet iudicandi, neque cuiquam de eius liceat iudicare iudicio. Siquidem ad illam de qualibet mundi parte appellandum est: ab illa autem nemo est appellare permissus. Sed nec illa preterimus, quod apostolica sedes sine ulla precedente sinodo et solvendi quos sinodus iniqua damnaverat, et damnandi, nulla existente sinodo, quos oportuit habuerit facultatem, et hoc nimirum pro suo principatu, quem B. Petrus apostolus Domini voce et tenuit semper et tenebit.' See Thiel, *Epistolae*, p. 309.

[2] Thus, e.g., Tancred, *Ordo* (MS. Caius Coll. 85, f. 7: 'Quis debet esse iudex ordinarius alicuius rei? Respondeo ille est iudex ordinarius rei apud quem ille reus domicilium habet. . . . Item Roma est patria omnium, ut ff. *ad munic*. l. *Roma* Dig. 50. 1, 33, et dominus papa iudex est ordinarius singulorum, ut ix. qu. iii. *cuncta per orbem* c. 17, C. 9, qu. 3.'

rescript, many of the advantages of central and of local justice can be combined. The court will sit in France or in England, and will be composed of Frenchmen or of Englishmen; but it will emanate from the supreme court and will wield prerogative powers.

Maintaining our assumed character as champions of federalism, let us observe how insidiously this procedure will sap the foundation of 'state rights.' The supreme ruler, the president of the federal community, becomes, in his own person or in the person of his commissioners, a judge competent to declare law in all cases and in all countries. And yet that patriotic sentiment which would be fretted by the presence of an Italian legate will lie dormant. English cases will be heard in England by Englishmen, though by Englishmen who derive their powers and instructions from Rome. It may come to this, that the natural protectors of 'state rights' will be constantly receiving and obeying mandates under which they act as the subordinate officials of the central tribunal. If this is to be so, we may as well give up all thought of federalism. At any rate the kind of jurisprudence which is the outcome of this judicial system is likely to be a centripetal, Romipetal[1] kind. It will not place in each diocesan or metropolitan church any general and indefinite power of declaring and making law within those wide limits that are drawn by federal interests; far rather it will suppose and construct an exhaustive *ius commune* for all causes in all lands, and merely allow that this 'common law' may be supplemented by the ordinances of 'inferior' prelates or varied by such local customs as are prescript and laudable.

But, to turn from these generalities to the particular case of England, I cannot but think, though there may

[1] Du Cange, s.v. *Romipeta*.

be something akin to impudence in my saying, that in the admirable books to which we are in the habit of looking for our English ecclesiastical history certain parts of the long and many-sided story receive too little notice. These happen to be the parts which interest me, for the omitted chapters are those which should deal with law and legal arrangements. In England the ecclesiastical historian is usually but little interested in law and legal arrangements. A meagre footnote will be the most that he will spare for an ecclesiastical code of some two thousand sections. The consequence is that many questions which seem grave to a student of law remain unanswered and even unasked. Is it not, for example, a grave question whether this theory that the pope is every man's ordinary bore fruit in England? Is it not a grave question whether in the age which saw the publication of the Decretals the ecclesiastical courts of first instance that did justice in this country were very often courts constituted for the occasion by a papal rescript? Answer these questions I cannot; ask them I can, and at the same time offer some reasons for thinking that an answer should not be lightly given.

In the first place, we may be quite certain that the theory which would give the pope an 'ordinary' jurisdiction in all ecclesiastical cases was well known in the England of Henry III.'s reign. Bracton has stated it.[1] There might, perhaps, be some force in the remark that Bracton was no canonist, and that, as a strenuous opponent of the claims of contemporary high churchmen, he was concerned to belittle the power of the English bishops in favour of the power of a pope who, provided

---

[1] Bracton, f. 412. 'In fine notandum de iurisdictione maiorum et minorum, et imprimis sicut dominus papa in spiritualibus super omnibus habeat ordinariam iurisdictionem, ita habet rex in regno suo ordinariam in temporalibus, et pares non habet neque superiores; et sunt qui sub eis ordinariam habent in multis, sed non ita meram sicut papa vel rex.'

that he could get money out of England, was willing that King Henry's justices should go their own way. But a much weightier piece of evidence is offered by this same Bracton. He has to speak at length of 'prohibitions' and to give models for the writs which are used for the purpose of keeping the ecclesiastical courts within their proper bounds. In so doing he habitually assumes that the suit which must be prohibited is being prosecuted under the authority of a papal rescript.¹ The records of his time show that this assumption had some warrant. We see one Englishman suing another Englishman before two or three papal delegates *per breve domini papae*, and we have no reason to believe that in all these instances there had already been an appeal to the pope from some inferior judge.² The newly published second volume of the Cartulary of St. Frideswide supplies us, if I am not mistaken, with records of no less than seventeen ecclesiastical lawsuits in which the priory was engaged between the years 1150 and 1240; all of them seem to be begun before papal commissioners; the English ordinaries are ignored.³

But some new light may be shed upon this matter by what remains to us of the work of William of Drogheda. Of him, therefore, let me say a few words. Little is known of his life, though his memory has been preserved for us by a famous chronicler, a famous canonist, and a house in the High Street of Oxford which still bears the name of Drawda Hall.⁴ Johannes

---

¹ Bracton, ff. 230b, 402b, 403, 403b, 404, 405.
² *Bracton's Note Book*, pll. 60, 192, 576, 1387, 1588; Prynne, *Records*, i. 12, 67, 69, &c.
³ There are a few suits of a later time which go to the English courts.
⁴ Mr. Hastings Rashdall, who has spoken of this hall in his admirable *Universities of Europe*, iii. 170, has kindly told me that the transfer of it took place in 1241. This appears from a copy at University College and a register at Queen's College.

Andreae, 'the fount and trumpet of the law,' reckons him among the number of those civilians who wrote books on procedure. While lecturing at Oxford he had, says the Bolognese doctor, composed a sufficiently praiseworthy and ample book *De Ordine Iudiciorum*, which was divided into six parts; it began by treating of 'impetration' (what 'impetration' means we shall see hereafter), and made a considerable use of the canonical sources.[1] From this we should infer that Johannes Andreae had seen the whole of a book of which but a small portion has come to our hands. Now praise from Johannes Andreae was praise indeed, and it has served at various times to awaken a faint interest in Drogheda and his doings.[2]

In the chronicle of Matthew Paris, Drogheda appears for one moment and then vanishes into the darkness. In 1241 the bishop of Coventry and Lichfield died. William of Montpellier was elected by the monks of the one church, but opposed by some of the canons of the other church and by the king. Litigation followed. Then, under the year 1245, we are told that he went to the pope and resigned his claim, having heard of the lamentable death of one who was his staunchest advocate in England: namely, William of Drogheda.[3]

[1] The passage is given by Savigny, *Geschichte* (ed. 1834), iii. 637, and by Schulte, *Geschichte*, ii. 353. 'Secundus vero sit Guilielmus de Droreda Anglicanus, qui legens Oxoniae satis commendabilem et copiosum libellum composuit de iudiciorum ordine, quem in sex partes divisit, et inchoavit ab impetrando; incipit autem: *Cum omne artificium*. In eo autem satis nostris iuribus utitur.' It seems clear from other passages that by 'nostra iura' Johannes meant the canon as distinguished from the civil law.

[2] Albericus Gentilis, *Laudes Academiae* (Hanoviae, 1605), p. 39: 'et Guilielmus Dorohius ... erat doctissimus et illustris academiae huius professor.'

[3] Mat. Par. *Chron. Mai.* iv. 423: 'Willelmus cognomento de Monte Pessulano ... cum audisset quod Magister Willelmus de Drouhedale *al.* Droghedale lugubriter expirasset, qui suus fuerat diligentissimus advocatus in Anglia ... doluit quod electus unquam exstitisset.' Whether

This seems a high testimony to Drogheda's ability: the elect bishop abandons all hope of success when he learns that his 'leading counsel' is dead. In the March of this same year Drogheda obtained papal letters suffering him to hold an additional benefice; therein he is described as rector of Strastun, in the diocese of Lincoln: that is, apparently, of Stratton Audley, in Oxfordshire.[1] That he wrote his book in 1239 or thereabouts is fairly well proved by the dates and the citations that occur in it.[2]

Portions of William's *Summa* are preserved in two manuscripts now belonging to Caius College, and in others which are at Laxemburg, Tours, and the Vatican.[3] We learn from the preface that the *Summa* consisted of six books. The first dealt with the procedure in an action down to litiscontestation; the second with matters occurring between litiscontestation and sentence; the third with sentence and its consequences; the fourth with appeal; the fifth with matrimonial causes; the sixth with criminal procedure and also with election and postulation. None of the manuscripts that I have

the 'lugubriter' implies an especially tragic death we can hardly say. An Englishman would easily believe that the name Drogheda should end in *dale*.

[1] *Calendar of Papal Registers*, i. 214. Here the name appears as Droweda.

[2] Some extracts from it were given in *English Historical Review*, xii. 645.

[3] Of the Caius MSS. tidings were given by Wunderlich in 1842 (*Zeitschrift für geschichtl. Rechtswissenschaft*, xi. 79). Bethmann-Hollweg, who had examined the Luxemburg MS. (*Stadtbibliothek*, No. 105), describes the work in *Civilprozess des gemeinen Rechts*, vi. 123. See also Schulte, *Geschichte*, ii. 113. For the Tours MS., see Dorange, *Catalogue des Manuscrits de la Bibliothèque de Tours*, p. 310. For the Vatican MS., see Stevenson, *Codices Palatini Latini Bibliothecae Vaticanae*, p. 283. Mr. Bliss has kindly given me some information about this Roman codex. See also Delisle, *Littérature latine*, p. 97. I owe my best thanks to the master and fellows of Caius College for permitting me to use their manuscripts.

mentioned contains the whole of the treatise thus projected. The longer of the Cambridge MSS. breaks off while the defendant is still propounding his 'exceptions,' while the other breaks off at a yet earlier point, when the plaintiff is composing his 'libel.' In neither of these cases, therefore, have we even the whole of the first of the six books. Yet the fragment offered by the longer codex is by no means brief. It fills with double columns a hundred pages of parchment, and there are some fifty lines on the page. The whole treatise, if it was ever finished, must have been ponderous. Its author could be verbose. His one modern critic, Bethmann-Hollweg, found little good to say of him.[1]

In a certain sense his book is academic: that is, it was meant in the first instance for the Oxford law school. On the other hand, it is intensely practical. He is going to teach his readers to win causes, and begs that a few of the fees that they earn may purchase masses for his soul. His object is to trace an action through all its stages, to solve the questions about procedure which will beset the practitioner, to supply him with useful formulas or models for the various documents which he may have to indite, and to offer him sound advice in the shape of *cautelae*. This last word we can hardly translate without condescending to the slang of 'tips,' and 'wrinkles,' and 'dodges'; and in truth some of William's *cautelae* do not deserve very pretty names, for they are none too honest. He was, I suppose, according to the standard of his time a learned man. He can finish almost every sentence with an appeal to Digest or Code, Decretum or Decretals; but,

---

[1] Bethmann-Hollweg, *op. cit.* p. 126: 'Von der Schrift selbst ist nicht viel Gutes zu sagen. Die Redseligkeit und Eitelkeit des Verfassers tritt schon darin hervor, dass er sich erst in einem kurzeren Vorwort und dann in einer längeren Vorrede über Absicht und Plan seiner Arbeit höchst weitschweifig auslässt.'

except in a few instances, we find none of those citations of other men's opinions which swell and swamp the work of the later canonists. However, it would appear that he took many of his formulas for *libelli* (or, as we might say, 'statements of claim') from a certain Roaldus or Redwaldus, whose name has been vainly sought in the histories of Savigny, Schulte, and Bethmann-Hollweg. He is well aware that of some of these formulas no use can be made in England; any attempt to employ them would at once call down a royal prohibition. In one of his *cautelae* he tells us that in England you cannot sue a layman for money in the ecclesiastical court, unless the cause be matrimonial or testamentary; but he goes on to explain that practically you can gain your end by nominally asking that the defendant may be chastened for his soul's health, since he will be unable to obtain absolution until he restores anything that he is wrongfully withholding. When we look at the large number of formulas for *libelli* of all sorts and kinds which William gives, we are reminded that he lives at Oxford in the midst of a privileged society. This is brought home to us yet more forcibly when in an amusing *cautela* he tells how one of his scholars was imprisoned by the mayor of Oxford, and how that miserable townsman found that no less than five actions based on this one rash deed were brought against him before an university which seems to have been both plaintiff and judge.

What we have of his work is perhaps too fragmentary and too technical to deserve an edition in the England of to-day. But one remarkable feature it has. William assumes that the first step taken by any English litigant will be the 'impetration' of a papal writ appointing judges delegate to hear his cause. This 'impetration,' he says, is the head and foundation of the whole procedure, and therefore the first formula that he gives us must be a precedent for a letter sent to the court of Rome by a plaintiff who is about to bring an action. This formula supposes that the vicar of a church has a complaint to make about tithes, oblations, or other matters against the rector and certain other persons, and that the plaintiff is desirous that the cause should be delegated to the dean, precentor, and archdeacon of Hereford. Such formulas the practitioner will keep in stock, and he will be careful to insert a '*si non omnes* clause' which will empower some of the judges to proceed in the absence of their fellows. The plaintiff is advised to retain a copy of this petition; also to entrust the petition not to one bearer but to several bearers, since there is a chance that one may die on the road. Moreover, if he has an adversary in the court at Rome, he had better see that he has a friend there also. This is not *dolus malus*, it is *dolus bonus*. If his 'impetration' is successful, then his next step will be to present the papal mandate to the delegates who are named in it, and to obtain from them a sealed memorandum acknowledging their receipt of it.

This procedure is strikingly similar to that which is open to an Englishman who wishes to bring an action in the English king's court. In either case we begin by 'impetrating' a writ.[1] In the one case it comes from the English, in the other from the Roman chancery. The same technical term is in use. The English serjeants will call the writ which starts an action 'the original.' William of Drogheda uses this very phrase. The plaintiff is to present 'the original' to the judges delegate.[2] Drogheda knows well enough that England

---

[1] See, e.g., Bracton, f. 253*b*: 'facta igitur impetratione.'

[2] 'Deinde videndum est quod ad officium actoris pertineat si velit quod adversarius eius vocetur ad iudicium. Accedat ad iudicem, nec exspectet

is full of judges ordinary; but he assumes and steadily maintains the assumption that all the big and remunerative litigation, all the litigation in which Oxford doctors are likely to have a professional interest, will be litigation which is brought in the first instance to a court constituted for that occasion by a papal *breve*.[1]

When we think of high seas and high Alps, and the dangers that beset the medieval wayfarer, we may marvel at the preference thus shown for a procedure which begins with a tedious, toilsome, and perilous journey, undertaken by the two or three bearers of a petition to a foreign prelate. Why not be content with the courts at home, where there was an archdeacon always at hand and the bishop's official was never many miles away? Part of our answer to this question will probably be that appeals had been so much encouraged that to go to the highest court in the first instance was often a short cut. Sooner or later the cause would be laid before the pope, and therefore time and money might be saved by at once seeking the threshold of the apostles and 'impetrating' an appointment of delegates.

In the second place, it is likely that the geographical limits set to diocesan justice were obstacles which often stood in a litigant's way. You wish to sue as co-defendants a man who lives at Lincoln and another who lives at York. What are you going to do? No English prelate has power over both these men. In the judicial system Canterbury is a unit and York is a unit; but

ut iudex ad eum ueniat, . . . et ostendat originale una cum memorando prius confecto ut supra dictum est, quia aliter iudex non crederet ei.' . . . 'Instruat iudicem de citacione facta per originale rescriptum domini pape et non per eius exemplum.'

[1] Does not this go even beyond the Italian models? Aegidius de Fuscariis (MS. Caius College, No. 54) begins his 'ordo' thus: 'Quoniam actores *plerumque* omisso ordinario iudice impetrant litteras volentes litigare sub iudice delegato, idcirco videndum est qualiter litterae debeant iudici presentari.'

S

England is no unit. Too often we speak of 'the church of England,' and forget that there was no ecclesiastically organised body that answered to that name. No tie of an ecclesiastical or spiritual kind bound the bishop of Chichester to the bishop of Carlisle, except that which bound them both to French and Spanish bishops. On the other hand, papal justice knew no geographical bounds, at least in the Occident. Drogheda in some of his formulas supposes that the dean and precentor of Hereford, who are the delegates appointed by the pope, will order the dean of Oxford to do this, that, and the other, as if he were their subordinate officer, and will threaten him with punishment if he does not obey.

But, thirdly, and this is of great importance, the plaintiff who went to the pope for a writ seems to have enjoyed a large liberty of choosing his own judges. In the letter of 'impetration' that he sent to Rome he named the persons whose appointment he desired. The pope, no doubt, was free to name other delegates in their stead; still we may believe that the plaintiff generally got his way unless he asked for something outrageous. And we have to remember that the defendant, unless he was one of those great people who kept permanent agents in the court of Rome, had no chance of being heard at this stage of the action, for indeed no action had yet been begun. A plaintiff, it is true, would, if well advised, be cautioned against asking for delegates who would be allied to him by any gross and obvious bonds, for the defendant would be able to 'recuse' judges against whom a specific charge of presumable partiality could be made; but still it is an enormous advantage for us to be able to select our judges, even though our choice be limited to those who are open to no 'exception.' About the time when Drogheda was lecturing, England was honoured by the presence of an Italian lawyer who was then serving our king, but was to become in aftertime a very prince amongst canonists, for, though Ostia has had many bishops, he, and only he, was to be 'Hostiensis.' He quitted England. He was going to buy a bishopric with money that he had embezzled, says Matthew Paris, who thought ill of Italians.¹ His own story is different. Our jealousy expelled him. An Englishman who has aught against a foreigner 'impetrates' from the pope the appointment of English judges, and, this being so, England is no place for foreigners.² Archbishop Peckham, when he was quarrelling with the bishop of Hereford, sent to his proctors at Rome a list of the judges who would be 'good,' of those who would be 'better,' of those who would be 'best'; and in the eyes of a litigant the most impartial judge will not be the 'best.'³

This, then, is the legal doctrine which was being taught in Oxford some five or six years after Gregory IX. had issued his code. It was being taught in an Oxford which was full of intellectual life while Edmund of Abingdon ruled at Canterbury and Robert Grosseteste at Lincoln. It was being taught in an Oxford, an England, which did not love the pope, but growled and grumbled at him and his exactions. The clergy were between the upper and nether millstones, and yet a revolt against the pope was impossible, for a revolt—at

¹ Mat. Par. *Chron. Maj.* iv. 33, 286, 351, 353. Compare Prynne, *Records*, ii. 578, 588, 590, 593, 632.
² Hostiensis, *Summa*, tit. 'de recus. iud. del.' (ed. Venet. 1605, col. 308) 'Consuevit etiam livor invidiae regnare inter indigenas et alienigenas. . . . Haec causa et quaedam aliae fecerunt me Angliam elongare. . . . Si Anglicus impetrat Anglicum contra alienigenam morantem in Anglia vel alienigenam compatriotam Anglicum, puto quod tum ratione familiaritatis et amicitiae quasi fraternae . . . tum ratione livoris invidiae, nisi sit persona valde honesta, talis iudex poterit recusari.'
³ Peckham's *Register*, p. 280.

all events an ecclesiastical revolt—must have a principle behind it, and will not be the outcome of mere grievances. Every principle that the pope could demand was being conceded to him by those who had the fate of the English church in their hands. Nor must we throw all the blame, if blame there is to be, upon the canonists, upon such men as William of Drogheda. In our own day and country the medieval canonist is defenceless; he has left no heirs. Some of us do not like lawyers; some of us do not like priests; upon the man who was half priest, half lawyer, many dislikes are concentrated. But we must be just to him. He was only drawing practical inferences from premisses that he shared with the theologian. Drogheda merely registers the fact that the pope is the universal 'ordinary' in order that he may teach his pupils how fame and fees are won. It is Grosseteste, the theologian, the bishop, the immortal Lincolniensis, who will preach with fervour the doctrine that the whole of a bishop's power is derived from, or at all events through, the pope, and thus make all thought of federalism an impiety. The bishop shines with a reflected light which will pale and vanish whenever the papal sun arises.[1]

To discover how many cases were carried in the first instance before the pope's delegates, and how many

[1] Grosseteste, *Epistolae*, 389: 'Quemadmodum igitur sol, quia non potest ubique super terram simul et semel praesentialiter lucere, ad tenebrarum purgationem et terrae nascentium vegetationem, ne aliquando tamen careat aliqua pars orbis terrarum solatio luminis, de plenitudine luminis sui, nullo per hoc sibi diminuto, lunam et stellas illuminat, ut in eius absentia luceant in firmamento caeli et illuminent terram ; ipsoque sole revertente et suam exhibente praesentiam super terram, ipsa minora luminaria radiis solis abscondita solari cedunt lumini : Ita dominus papa, respectu cuius omnes alii praelati sunt sicut luna et stellae, suscipientes ab ipso quicquid habent potestatis ad illuminationem et vegetationem ecclesiae. . . .' *Ibid.* p. 369 : 'Si dominus papa, qui a Iesu Christo, cuius vicem gerit, recepit plenitudinem postestatis. . . . Si episcopus potestatem quam accepit a domino papa et a Iesu Christo per domini papae mediationem. . . .'

went to the English ordinaries, would be difficult. We hardly as yet know where to look for the original records (*acta*) which deal with the doings of the delegates. Apparently there was no reason why such records should be carefully preserved in large numbers, for they were records of courts which had no permanent existence, but were dissolved so soon as a single cause had been decided. The quest, however, would not be hopeless, and anyone who is exploring this tract of history might at the same time explore another and contiguous region of which too little is known. We have good reason to believe that the 'usurpations' of the court of Rome were reproduced on a diminished scale by the usurpations of the court of Canterbury. What is done by the great pope of Rome is imitated in humble fashion by our own little homely pope, who is indeed *alterius orbis papellus*. If the one would make his court a court of first instance for the whole of the Christian world, the other would make his court a court of first instance for the whole of his province.

In 1282, as is well known, a fierce dispute broke out between John Peckham, the archbishop of Canterbury, and Thomas Cantilupe, the bishop of Hereford.[1] To all appearance Peckham asserted for himself and his official (1) a general right to entertain in the first instance complaints made against his suffragans' subjects (*subditi*), and (2) a general right to entertain appeals *omisso medio*: in other words, to hear appeals brought to him directly from the courts of the bishops' subordinates: for example, the courts of the archdeacons. The archbishop excommunicated the bishop. The bishop appealed to Rome, and died in Italy while prosecuting his suit. Forthwith he worked miracles, and in due

---

[1] Peckham's *Register*, pp. 269, 271, 278, 290, 299, 308, 315, 318, 321, 328, 334, 337, 382, 393.

course became a saint. From this canonisation of one who very probably was absolved only at the hour of death we may infer that the court of Rome was inclined to take a not unfavourable view of his resistance to the archiepiscopal pretensions.[1] Meanwhile, however, Peckham's action had aroused a general opposition among his suffragans. They presented a list of one-and-twenty grievances, each of which consisted in some unjustifiable (so they said) extension of the metropolitan jurisdiction.[2] To every article the archbishop returned a haughty and unyielding reply. He was in the right; his reverend brethren were in the wrong.[3] Soon afterwards, however, he consented to submit some of the disputed questions to five referees chosen by himself as being men exceptionally learned in the rights and customs of the church of Canterbury.

It is hardly too much to say that at every important point they found that the archbishop or his official had been innovating.[4] Two of their decisions are especially worthy of notice. The first of these is as follows:—

> Whereas the official of the court of Canterbury in modern times has, in cases in which no appeal was being made, issued rescripts upon the complaint of the subjects of the suffragans more frequently than was done by the officials of the archbishop's predecessors, since it appears that some of the older officials but rarely and some never at any time issued rescripts upon such complaints, we decide that no rescripts shall be issued upon such complaints in time to come.

An exception was made for cases of 'perplexity,'—that is, for cases in which the courts of the suffragans could

---

[1] *Acta Sanctorum*, 2 Oct. The bull of canonisation (p. 507) says: 'Iura vero suae ecclesiae defensabat indutus iustitia ut lorica.' The opinion of the papal commissaries as to the excommunication will be found at p. 594. At the head of the commission was William Durant, the nephew of the famous Speculator and himself a canonist of repute.
[2] Peckham's *Register*, p. 328.   [3] *Ibid.* p. 332.
[4] *Ibid.* p. 33.

not, owing to **the geographical limitation of** their competence, do full **justice,—but the** general **rule seems to** mean that the archbishop is not to make his **court a court of first instance for the folk who dwell outside** his diocese though inside his province.¹ An **abuse has been** growing **up;** its growth must be checked. **One of the** roots of **that** abuse is **laid bare by another decree of the referees.**

Albeit the archbishop, by **virtue of his** legation, has, so it seems, power to issue rescripts **upon the complaint of** [his suffragans' subjects] where there is no **appeal, still this power is** not extended **to the archbishop's official, since the extraordinary legatine** jurisdiction **is not** included in the **ordinary jurisdiction of** the officialty, **even though the archbishop when appointing an official has** willed that **it should be so** included. **Otherwise we should have the absurdity that a legate could** avail himself of the **services of an official just as if his power were** [not **extraordinary,** but] **ordinary. Therefore we decree that the officials of Canterbury are not to issue rescripts upon such complaints as aforesaid by virtue of the legatine power; but if the archbishop** [himself] **desires to issue rescripts in his character as legate he may, so it seems, do this if some reasonable and specially urgent cause requires it, provided that he does not intend to prejudice the rights of his suffragans and their churches.**

Very cautiously **and with a repeated** *ut videtur* **these** learned **persons are willing to admit that as legate the archbishop may enjoy some jurisdiction of first instance, but he ought to be chary in his use of it, and he cannot delegate it in a lump to his official.² Having received this report, drawn up by men whom he had selected, Peckham in a none too gracious letter told his suffragans that he would make concessions and waive some of his rights.³**

¹ The typical case of 'perplexity' was that which engendered the doctrine of 'prerogative probate.' As to this see Lyndwood, p. 174; also the bull of Alexander VI. in Wilkins, *Concilia*, iii. 645.

² They would not, I take it, have denied that 'delegatus principis potest delegare,' in case only one particular suit were delegated; but the subdelegation of an 'universitas causarum' was a different matter.

³ Peckham's *Register*, p. 334.

If, therefore, as our books teach us, the court of the archbishop had before the end of the middle ages become not only 'the court of appeal from all the diocesan courts of the province,' but also 'a court of first instance in all ecclesiastical matters,' we can hardly escape the inference that since Peckham's day it had gone on usurping and usurping jurisdiction.[1] In such a context the word 'usurpation' will not of necessity imply anything that is wrong. Many an excellent arrangement has its origin in usurpation. The king's courts of common law were notable usurpers. Were it not for usurpation, England might still be feudal. Only let us not keep one measure for the pope and another for the archbishop. Neither the one nor the other had much regard for the rights of mere bishops. The statutory Reformation of the English church began with an act that was aimed not at Rome but at Canterbury.[2]

Usurpation we see wherever we turn. If we say that the medieval church was a state, we must add that among medieval states it was not the least anarchical. True that in the matter of mere bloodshed it could not compete with the temporal states, but the eternity, the costliness, the rancour of its internal quarrels were unmatched in the annals of secular principalities. In every zone of the hierarchy from the utmost to the inmost

---

[1] *Ecclesiastical Courts Commission*, i. p. xx : 'It was the court of appeal from all the diocesan courts of the province, and likewise (whether or not by virtue of the archbishop's legatine capacity) a court of first instance in all ecclesiastical matters.' These words were taken from the paper written by Dr. Stubbs, *ibid.* p. 31. Lyndwood, pp. 277, 278, urges with some vehemence that the archiepiscopal official can wield the legatine as well as the ordinary jurisdiction. This is directly contrary to the award of Peckham's referees. Lyndwood seems to be asserting his right as official against the claims of the archbishop's 'auditors.'

[2] Stat. 23 Hen. VIII. c. 9 : 'An Act that no person shall be cited out of the diocese where he or she dwelleth, except in certain cases.' See Warham's protest, Wilkins, *Concilia*, iii. 746.

there were open questions of constitutional law which, if they were to be closed at all, could only be closed by persistent and relentless usurpation. Claims to jurisdictional superiority were being urged which had behind them no principle except that which recognises the accomplished fact, and they were met by proofs of a resistance in the past which would justify a resistance in the future. It will be enough to refer to the disputes about primacies, of which our own country displays a notorious example. This is but a typical case. In the golden age of ecclesiastical law a man might say : 'Well, I've been in some big affairs in my time. I was counsel for the archbishop of Bourges when he claimed a primacy over the archbishop of Bordeaux. I was counsel for Compostella when it resisted Toledo's claim to a primacy over all Spain. I was counsel for the archbishop of Pisa when he claimed a primacy over Sardinia.'[1] But let us think what this would mean if we translated it into modern and secular terms. Will the North American colonies ever unite in a federal system if through a long age Maine, for example, has been asserting for its court a bitterly contested right to hear appeals from all the courts of New England? At the growth of the court of Rome's judicial power we cease to wonder when we see how uncertain, how hotly debated are the boundaries

---

[1] 'Vidi tamen contencionem inter Bituricensem et Burdegalensem qui dicebat se primatem Burdegalensis et fui advocatus pro Bituricensi coram domino Gregorio IX. Item dicit se primatem Toletanus tocius Yspanie et vidi contencionem inter illum et Compostelanum coram domino Gregorio IX. et fui advocatus pro Compostelano. Item dicit se primatem tocius Anglie archiepiscopus Cantuariensis et contendit de hoc cum Eboracensi. Item dicit se archiepiscopus Pisanus tocius Sardinie et fui advocatus pro eo coram domino Gregorio IX.' This comes from a treatise contained in MS. Caius Coll. No. 54, which treatise begins thus : 'Super actionibus communibus compositi sunt libelli per graciam Iesu Christi que de iure civili fuerant invente seu de iure pretorio, puta de edictis et interdictis.' This seems to be the work of Roffredus (Savigny, cap. 40, § 67 ; Schulte, ii. 75).

which mark off the spheres proper to the other courts. The choice lay between anarchy and the *plenitudo potestatis*.

That the English church did less than other churches towards the unification of the universal church, towards the consolidation of the judicial, and therewith the legislative, might of the popes, we shall not easily believe if we have glanced at the decretals. Just at the critical moment England seems to have demanded, or at anyrate to have received, a far larger number of papal mandates than would have fallen to her lot, had the supply that was exported from Rome been equitably distributed among the importing countries according to their area or their population. For a reason that deserves statement, it is difficult for us to arrive at precise figures. The compiler of Pope Gregory's statute book has in most cases endeavoured to preserve, in the form of a superscription to each decretal, not only the name of the pope who issued it, but also the title of the prelate to whom it was sent. Thus, for example, it is a decretal sent by Alexander III. to the archbishop of York: *Alexander III. Eboracensi archiepiscopo*. In the course of transcription, however, these titles have suffered badly, as anyone may see who looks at the variants given at the foot of the pages in Friedberg's edition. Thus it will often be doubtful whether a certain rescript was directed to London, to Lund, to Lyons, or to Laon. The copyists take little care about this matter, because in their eyes it is so trivial. What difference can it make whether this decretal was sent to York or to Evreux, to Lincoln or to Langres? It contains a rule of law, of catholic and supernational law.

As to the proper names which occur in the decretal itself, these have often been defaced beyond hope of recognition. Here, for example, is a missive which deals with a lawsuit between two English parsons. The parish of the one is variously designated as Sander, Santer, Santen, **Sandeia**, Sandria, Sandinia, **Sandeta**, Sandaia, Fand., Sandola; that of the other as **Pelen**, Pele, Petel, Ploren., **Pelin.**, **Peleren.**, Pelerenen., Positione, Posittoni, Pon., **Porni**, **Peieren.**, Poinone, Portione, Pone, Portino, Porten, Potton.[1] Anyone who for his sins has endured the railway journey between Oxford and Cambridge will guess that the one village is Sandy, and the other Potton; but to the decretist the whereabouts of these places was less than nothing. They might be in Spain; they might be in Hungary; they might be nowhere. They were but Blackacre and Whiteacre, and the two quarrelsome parsons were but Titius and Maevius, Styles and Nokes; but they have succeeded in extracting from Alexander III. a judgment which the Italian lawyers think worthy of preservation, and which, when the *partes decisae* have been omitted from it, finds a place in the Gregorian law-book.

Therefore it is easy to make mistakes; but we shall not go very far wrong if we say that out of the 470 decretals of Alexander III. which received the sanction of Gregory IX., about 180 were directed to England.[2] Now it is true that during many years of his pontificate (1159-1181) Alexander was not in a position to send effectual decretals to those lands which obeyed the emperor, for Frederick was keeping anti-popes of his own. Also it may be true that the shifty and many-faced policy of our Henry II. was from time to time not unfavourable to papal interference with English affairs,

---

[1] c. 4, X. 2. 13.
[2] To take another test, we look at those letters of Alexander to which Jaffé could assign no date. We find about 430 (Nos. 8815-9245) addressed to persons whose names are given. About 212 of these were sent to England.

provided that those affairs were of a purely ecclesiastical kind. Unfortunately the majority of Alexander's decretals cannot be, or have not been, precisely dated, and about those which came to England we rarely know for certain whether they were issued before or after the king's quarrel with Becket, before or after the murder of the archbishop, before or after the humiliation at Avranches. But, explain it how we may, the fact that more than a third of Alexander's permanently important decretals have English cases for their subject-matter is, or ought to be, one of the most prominent facts in the history of the English church. As a maker of case law, Alexander is second to no pope, unless it be to Innocent III., and a surprisingly large number of the cases which evoke case law from these two mitred lawyers are English cases.

A decretal is by no means always the decision of a concrete case; often it is an abstract answer to an abstract question. The English bishops seem to have been peculiarly fond of submitting such questions to the pope. What, they ask, are we to do about this or that matter? In 1204 the bishop of Ely sent a whole legal catechism to Innocent III. The answering epistle[1] has been cut up into no less than thirteen *capitula*, which are included in the Gregorian book. The bishop wants answers to the following questions:—How is he to tell authentic from spurious decretals?[2] Can a man who has been received into the subdiaconate without imposition of hands be allowed to minister? Must the rite of confirmation be repeated when by mistake it has been performed with oil instead of chrism?[3] In what cases should a peremptory day be given to a defendant for his dilatory exceptions?[4] In what cases must

---

[1] Potthast, *Regesta*, No. 2350; *Innocentii Opera* (Migne), ii. 478.
[2] c. 8, X. 2. 22.   [3] c. 1, X. 1. 16.   [4] c. 4, X. 2. 25.

litigants appear in person?¹ Can a papal delegate compel another person to act as sub-delegate? Is a partial sub-delegation of a cause possible? What is to to be done when one set of papal delegates has been overruled by another set, an appeal having been excluded by the commission that appointed the first set, but having none the less been entertained? Must the ordinary execute a sentence that he knows to be unjust if commanded to do so by the papal delegate who has passed the sentence? What is to be done if the delegate has appointed a day for trial, and one of the parties maliciously procures that the delegate shall be summoned elsewhere by the king or the archbishop, so that his absence may cause delay?² Who is to decide whether one delegation has been revoked by a later delegation, the first or the second set of delegates?³ When a cause has come to the archbishop by way of appeal, can he compel a subject of one of his suffragans to act as delegate? If a sentence of excommunication has been pronounced by a papal delegate, and the delegate dies, can anyone absolve the excommunicate without a special mandate from the pope?⁴ May a man deduct necessary expenses before he tithes the produce of mills or fisheries?⁵ When the religious under papal privilege have been suffered to appropriate a church to their use, and the parson dies, may they take possession without waiting for episcopal induction?⁶ *Quid iuris* if a lay patron presents a clerk, and the bishop refuses to admit him, and he appeals to the pope, and the patron presents another clerk, whom the bishop institutes?⁷ If a bishop, with the consent of the patron, confers a church upon the religious, saying

¹ c. 14, X. 2. 1.   ² c. 28, X. 1. 29.   ³ c. 14, X. 1. 3.
⁴ c. 11, X. 1. 31.   ⁵ c. 28, X. 3. 30.   ⁶ c. 16, X. 3. 33.
⁷ c. 29, X. 3. 38.

simply, 'We grant you that church,' do the religious acquire the church itself or merely the patronage?[1] Can a bishop, without the consent of the pope or of his chapter, confer the obventions of a parish church upon a religious house?[2] When the words of a rescript exclude an appeal, are they to be read as excluding all appeals, or merely such as are frivolous?[3]

We must admire the patience of Pope Innocent, who, though not without the remark that he had many other things to do, set himself down to answer this lengthy examination paper, and in so doing to declare the law of the universal church. But as Englishmen, we may be more interested in the bishop's questions than in the pope's answers, and they certainly show a docility which, whether praiseworthy or blameworthy, is remarkable enough, especially if we remember that Eustace of Ely was an important member of the English state as well as of the English church. If the pope acquired an almost unlimited power of declaring law, if all the important spiritual causes passed out of the hands of the 'ordinary' judges into the hands of papal delegates, the bishops of England were more responsible for this good or bad result than were the bishops of any other country.

We may be the more surprised at the frequency with which our prelates went to the pope for their law, if we observe that they sometimes received in return a smart rebuke. Archbishop Richard of Canterbury (1174–1184) has taken Pope Alexander's opinion about the absolution of a certain litigant. The answering decretal begins with the cheerful words *Qua fronte*.[4]

With what face you dare to consult us about questions of law we cannot understand, since you are said to be perverting the order of

---

[1] c. 7, X. 3. 24.   [2] c. 9, X. 3. 10.
[3] c. 53, X. 2. 28.   [4] c. 25, X. 2. 28.

justice in matters which are plain and free of doubt, and are obviously infringing that ecclesiastical liberty for which your predecessor, the glorious martyr Thomas, was not afraid to suffer martyrdom. You are said to be confirming the election of bishops, not in a church, as is canonical and becoming, nor even in your palace or your chamber, but in the very chamber of the king, against the rule of law, and against the dignity of the pontifical office.

To consult a superior who would speak to you in this fashion cannot always have been a pleasant task, yet apparently it had to be performed. Better this, perhaps, than to have your judgments overruled on appeal, as they would be if they fell behind the last new law that the popes had evolved. The decent pomp of ecclesiastical correspondence will be preserved. All bishops are the pope's 'venerable brothers.' Open threats will rarely be uttered, will rarely be necessary. A quiet 'Don't let us have to write a second time' will usually be enough.[1] But on occasion a threat will be added. If, says Alexander to the archbishop of Canterbury and his suffragans, you presume to infringe this our command, we, with the Lord's authority, will quash your proceedings, and gravely punish your disobedience.[2]

Already in the twelfth century appeals to Rome had become frequent. It is a common story that English litigants have either by their proctors or in their proper persons made their way to the papal court. But already many of the English causes that are laid before this supreme tribunal seem to be causes that have never come before any lower court. The pope rarely decided them. Far more commonly he delegated them to two or three English prelates. The cause was heard in England; but in more than one way this arrangement must have brought home to our bishops a consciousness

---

[1] c. 9, X. 3. 5. 'Alexander III. Cantuarensi archep scopo ... ita quod ... nos propter hoc iterato tibi scribere non compellamur.
[2] c. 3, X. 1. 14.

of their subordinate position. For one thing, they could not refuse to act as delegates; they could not refuse even to act as sub-delegates. It was a special privilege of the *princeps*—that is, of the pope—that his delegates could make delegates. Then in many cases they received careful instructions for their procedure. Only the bare question of fact was left to them. They are told that if they find that certain allegations are true, they are to pass a certain sentence. Again, the pope was free to choose such prelates as would give effect to his opinions. Thus, for example, Alexander III. seems to have been fond of the abbot of Ford, who otherwise would not have stood very high in the roll of English abbots.[1] Lastly, what we may call the natural order of the English church is always being inverted; the last becomes first, the first last when the pope pleases. A cause which concerns the archbishop of Canterbury will be committed to some of his suffragans, or (and this must be still more galling) to the rival primate.

The same thing happens when there is no mere appeal from the metropolitan, but a complaint of wrongful behaviour against him. Thus is he addressed by Alexander:[2]—

A certain clerk, R. by name, the bearer of these presents, has complained to us that, while he was studying in the schools, you, not having cited him, despoiled him of the church of W. without judgment; and therefore, because it is not meet that you should despoil

---

[1] He seems to be addressed in c. 9, X. 2. 13; c. 3, X. 2. 14; c. 7, X. 2. 20; c. 7, X. 3. 38; c. 4, X. 4. 17; c. 5, X. 4. 17. During Alexander's time Ford had one distinguished abbot, namely, Baldwin, who became bishop of Worcester in 1180, and archbishop of Canterbury in 1185. In the *Guisborough Cartulary*, ii. 81, we have a decretal sent to him by Alexander. The bishop of Chichester, the abbot of Evesham, and B., abbot of Ford, are to hear a cause between the canons of Guisborough and the archbishop of York.

[2] c. 7, X. 2. 13.

the clerks within your jurisdiction of **their benefices** without reasonable and manifest cause, since you are bound to make paternal provision for them, we by apostolic writ order and command that, if this be so, you restore to the said clerk the said church, with the **revenues** thence received, and allow him to possess the same in peace; and, **when** the restitution has been made, then, if you have anything **to** urge against him in the matter of the said church, you can in your **own** person, or by a sufficient representative, bring an action in **due** form **against** the said R. before our venerable brother the bishop **of** Exeter, **our** delegate, and you are to receive and obey **his sentence,** for we have committed the **cause to the said** bishop.

The metropolitan **must plead as plaintiff before the** suffragan, the superior **before the inferior, if the *princeps* will** have it so.

All this was happening just at the time when the popes were laying the practical foundation for the gigantic edifice of express statute law that was to be reared in the thirteenth century. The theoretic foundation had been laid; we may see it in Gratian's Decretum. Whether the theory would become fact, that was the question. What was requisite, if the pope was to legislate on a grand scale, was a settled practical habit of looking to Rome for declarations of the 'common law' of the church. If that habit were once formed, the fine line which divides the declaration of law from open legislation might easily be crossed. The sharp distinction which nowadays we draw between the function of the judge and the function of the law-maker was but slowly emerging, and was less likely to emerge in the ecclesiastical than in the temporal sphere. That distinction only becomes sharp when the two functions are performed by two organs, and the drift towards monarchy which runs through the history of the church prevents any *séparation des pouvoirs*. What we see in the whole, we see in every part. The bishop is judge, governor, lawgiver. He becomes an inferior judge, an inferior governor, an inferior lawgiver; but all these functions are combined in his hand. What we see in the parts, we see in the whole. There will be no *séparation des pouvoirs*; there will be a *plenitudo potestatis*. Then, again, the authoritative answer given to abstract questions of law by an almost inspired jurisconsult, who derives from on high his *ius respondendi*, serves to mediate between the judgment and the statute, and thus his *obiter dicta* stand on much the same level with the *ratio decidendi*. If once there be formed a settled practical habit of looking to him for declarations of the law, all else will be easy. One small step will be taken by Innocent III., another small step by Honorius III.,— steps so small that only a vigilant criticism can detect them,[1]—and then Gregory IX. will issue a code of some two thousand sections. The Englishmen who gave Alexander III. the opportunity for issuing a hundred and eighty decretals of permanent importance contributed an ample share to the plenitude of power.

Did they question the binding force of those statute books which in a great measure were the outcome of their own submissiveness? Did they treat those books, not as statute books, but as reputable 'manuals'? I have been giving my reasons for thinking that what most Englishmen would regard as the pleasant answer to these questions is not true. As yet, however, a detailed history of our ecclesiastical courts is impossible. Very few attempts have been made to put in print the records out of which that history must be wrung. They are voluminous. In one which comes from the year 1285, and which is now lying before me, the sixty-fifth witness is giving evidence in a suit about tithes.[2]

---

[1] Schulte, *Geschichte*, i. 87, 90.
[2] Fragmentary record preserved in the library of Caius College, *Prioress of Wroxhall v. Abbot of Reading*.

Still what has been done for the temporal might be done for the spiritual courts, had anybody a mind to do it. Those who achieved the task would have to learn much that has not been taught in England during the past three centuries, and, it may be, to unlearn a good deal that has been taught too often. I have been trying in these papers to suggest that some questions of fundamental importance are still open, and thereby to arouse the spirit which copies legal records and prints them.[1]

[1] The issue of the papal law-books is singularly well attested by English chroniclers. Mat. Par. *Chron. Mai.* iii. 328. 'His quoque temporibus [1235] Gregorius Papa nonus, videns decretalium taediosam prolixitatem, sub quodam compendio eas eleganter abbreviatas et collectas sollenniter et autentice per totius mundi latitudinem legi praecepit et divulgari. Illas autem ab auctore ipsarum Gregorianas appellamus, sic incipientes, "Rex pacificus, etc."' Trivet (*Eng. Hist. Soc.*), p. 364: 'Papa Bonifacius constitutiones quasdam praedecessorum suorum extravagantes, adiectis quibusdam novis, in unum volumen redigi fecit, hoc anno; quod tertio die Maii coram consistorio lectum et approbatum constituit Sextum Decretalium appellari.' (Apparently the date should be 3rd March 1298; Schulte, *op. cit.* ii. 35.) Walsingham, i. 153: 'Hoc anno dominus Papa Septimum Librum Decretalium a praedecessore suo compositum, et quasi ab ipso deletum, promulgavit, instituit et confirmavit.' Sir John Davies in his *Reports* (ed. 1674), p. 716, tells of a manuscript of the Sext at New College, Oxford, bearing the following inscription: 'Anno Domini 1298, 19 Nov., in ecclesia fratrum praedicatorum Oxoniae fuit facta publicatio lib. 6 Decretalium.' This seems to show that the book was published in the university within a few months after its issue.

IV. HENRY II. AND THE CRIMINOUS CLERKS

If in this essay I venture to write a few words about the quarrel between Henry and Becket, a quarrel which has raged from their day until our own, it is with no intention of taking a side, still less with any hope of acting as a mediator. I have no wish to make myself a judge between the king and the archbishop, or between Freeman and Froude. But, so it seems to me, there is a certain question of fact, about which we are wont to suppose that there is and can be only one opinion, while in truth two different opinions are being entertained. Possibly I may do some good by showing that this is so. Perhaps if we were better agreed about the facts of the case, we should differ somewhat less about the merits of the disputants. At any rate, it is not well that we should think that we agree when really we disagree.

What did Henry II. propose to do with a clerk who was accused of a crime? This is a simple question, and every historian of England must answer it. Generally, so far as I can see, he finds no difficulty and feels no doubt. And yet, when I compare the answers given by illustrious and learned writers, I seem to see unconscious disagreement. The division list, if I were to state it, would be curious. Some of Henry's best friends would find themselves in the same lobby with warm admirers of Becket, and there would be great names on either side of the line. But I will not thus set historian against historian, for my purpose is not controversial, and I am very ready to believe that every writer has told so much of the truth as it was advisable that he should tell, regard being had to the scale of his work and the character of those for whom he wrote. Rather I would explain that, without doing much violence to the text, it is possible to put two different interpretations upon that famous clause in the Constitutions of Clarendon which deals with criminous clerks. I may be told that the difference is small, and hardly visible to any but lawyers. Still it may be momentous, for neither Becket nor Henry, unless both have been belied, was above making the most of a small point, or insisting on the letter of the law.

Let us have the clause before us:—

Clerici rettati et accusati de quacunque re, summoniti a iusticia regis vement in curiam ipsius, respousuri ibidem de hoc unde videbitur curiae regis quod ibidem sit respondendum, et in curia ecclesiastica unde videbitur quod ibidem sit respondendum; ita quod iusticia regis mittet in curiam sanctae ecclesiae ad videndum qua ratione res ibi tractabitur. Et si clericus convictus vel confessus fuerit, non debet de cetero eum ecclesia tueri.

Now, according to what seems to be the commoner opinion, we might comment upon this clause in some such words as these:—Offences of which a clerk may be accused are of two kinds. They are temporal or they are ecclesiastical. Under the former head fall murder, robbery, larceny, rape, and the like; under the latter, incontinence, heresy, disobedience to superiors, breach of ceremonial rules, and so forth. If charged with an offence of the temporal kind, the clerk must stand his trial in the king's court; his trial, his sentence will be like that of a layman. For an ecclesiastical offence, on the other hand, he will be tried in the court Christian. The king reserves to his court the right to decide what offences are temporal, what ecclesiastical; also he asserts the right to send delegates to view the doings of the spiritual tribunals.

The words, perhaps, are patient of this meaning. Nevertheless, if we adopt it, some questions will occur to our minds. Why should Henry care about what goes on in the ecclesiastical courts if those courts are only to deal with breaches of purely ecclesiastical rules? If he proposed to send his commissioners to watch trials for incontinence, simony, and the like, he inflicted a gratuitous and useless insult upon the tribunals of the church. And then let us look at the structure of the clause. In its last words it says that after a clerk has been convicted or has confessed, the church is no longer to protect him. Has been convicted of what? Has confessed what? Some temporal crime it must be. But the phrase which tells us this is divorced from all that has been said of temporal crimes. We have a clumsy sentence: 'A clerk, if accused of a temporal crime, is to be tried in the king's court; but if accused of an ecclesiastical offence, then he is to be tried in a spiritual court; and when he has confessed or been convicted [of a temporal crime], the church is no longer to protect him.' And what, if this interpretation be correct, is the meaning of the statement, that when he has confessed or been convicted the church is to protect him *no longer*? If he is to be tried like a layman in a temporal court, the church will never protect him at all.

Let us attempt a rival commentary. The author of this clause, though he may use very general words (*de quacunque re*), is not thinking of two different classes of misdeeds. The purely ecclesiastical offences are not in debate. No one doubts that for these a man, be he clerk or lay, will be tried in and punished by the spiritual court. He is thinking of the grave crimes, of murder and the like. **Now** every such crime is a breach of temporal law; **and it** is also a breach of the law of the church. **The** clerk who commits murder breaks the king's peace; but he also infringes the divine law, and—no canonist will doubt this—ought to **be** degraded. Very well. **A** clerk is accused of such a crime. He is summoned before the king's **court,** and he is to answer there—let us mark this word *respondere* —for what he ought to answer for there. What ought he to answer for there? The **breach** of the king's peace and the felony. When he has answered—when, that is, he has (to use the words of **the plea** roll) '**come** and defended the breach **of the** king's **peace,** and the felony, and the slaying, **and all** of it **word by** word,' then, without any trial, **he is to** be **sent to the** ecclesiastical **court.** In that court he must **answer as an ordained clerk** accused **of homicide, and in that court there will be a** trial (*res ibi tractabitur*). If this spiritual tribunal convicts him, it **will** degrade him, and thenceforth the church must no longer protect him. **He will be brought** back into the king's court—one **of the** objects **of sending** royal officers into the spiritual **court is to prevent** his **escape—and, having been** brought **back, no** longer a clerk but **a mere laymen, he will** be sentenced (probably without **any** further **trial) to the** layman's **punishment,** death or mutilation. **The scheme is** this: accusation and plea **in the temporal court; trial,** conviction, degradation **in the ecclesiastical court;** sentence **in the** temporal court to **the** layman's **punishment.**

This I believe **to** be the meaning **of the clause.** The contrary opinion suggests **itself** to **us because we** give to the **word** *respondere* a sense that it does not necessarily **bear.** No doubt if nowadays we say that a man must answer **for his crime at the Old** Bailey, we mean that he can be tried there and sentenced there.

But we ought not lightly to give to *respondere* so wide a meaning when it occurs in a legal document. It means to answer, 'to put in an answer,' to plead, 'to put in a plea.' The words of our clause are fully satisfied if the clerk, instead of being allowed to say, 'I am a clerk and will not answer here,' is driven to 'defend'—that is, to deny in set terms—the breach of the king's peace and the felony, and is then suffered to add, 'But I am a clerk, and can be tried only by the ecclesiastical forum.' According to this opinion, Henry did not propose that a clerk accused of crime should be *tried* in a temporal court, and he did not propose that a *clerk* should be punished by a temporal court. The clerk was to be tried in the bishop's court; the convict who was to be sentenced by the king's court would be no clerk, for he would have been degraded from his orders.

Even if this clause stood by itself, we should, so I venture to think, have good reason for accepting the second as the sounder of these two interpretations. If we look to the words, it seems the easier; if we look to the surrounding circumstances, it seems the more probable. But we do not want for contemporaneous expositions of it. In the first place, I will allege the letter addressed to the pope in the name of the bishops and clergy of the province of Canterbury:—

> Qua in re partis utriusque zelus enituit; episcoporum in hoc stante iudicio, ut homicidium, et si quid huiusmodi est, exauctoratione sola puniretur in clerico; rege vero existimante poenam hanc non condigne respondere flagitio, nec stabiliendae paci bene prospici, si lector aut acolythus quemquam perimat, ut sola iam dicti ordinis amissione tutus existat.[1]

According to this version of the story, there is no dispute between king and clergy as to the competence of any tribunal; the sole question is as to whether

[1] *Materials for the Hist. of Thomas Becket*, v. 405.

degradation—a punishment which can be inflicted only by the ecclesiastical court—is a sufficient penalty for such a crime as murder. Still more to the point are the words of Ralph de Diceto:—

> Rex Anglorum volens in singulis, ut dicebat, maleficia debita cum severitate punire, et ordinis dignitatem ad iniquum trahi compendium incongruum esse considerans, clericos a suis iusticiariis in publico flagitio deprehensos episcopo loci reddendos decreverat, ut quos episcopus inveniret obnoxios praesente iusticiario regis exauctoraret, et post curiae traderet puniendos.[1]

Now this is as plain a statement as could be wished that the second of our two interpretations is the right one, and that the accused clerk is to be tried by his bishop. Those therefore who contend for the contrary opinion seem bound to maintain that the Dean of St. Paul's did not know, or did not choose to tell, the truth. Still it may be said of one of these witnesses—the author of the letter to the pope—that he is Gilbert Foliot, Becket's bitter antagonist, and of the other that he may have had his version of the tale from Foliot, and that, though a fair-minded man, he was inclined to make the best case that he could for the king; and I must admit, or rather insist, that, in the last words of the passage which I have cited from him, Ralph de Diceto is making a case for the king, for he is in effect telling us by the phrase that is here printed in italics, that we ought to read our Gratian and see how strong the king's case is.

But we may turn to other accounts. In the tract known as *Summa Causae* the king is supposed to address the bishops thus :—

> Peto igitur et volo, ut tuo domine Cantuariensis et coepiscoporum tuorum consensu, clerici in maleficiis deprehensi vel confessi exauctorentur illico, et mox *curiae* meae lictoribus *tradantur*, ut omni defensione ecclesiae destituti corporaliter perimantur. Volo etiam et

[1] R. de Diceto, i. 313.

peto ut in illa exauctoratione de meis officialibus aliquem interesse consentiatis, ut exauctoratum clericum mox comprehendat, ne qua ei fiat copia corporalem vindictam effugiendi.¹

Thereupon 'the bishops,' who in this version take the king's side, urge that the demand is not unreasonable. *Episcopi dicebant secundum leges saeculi clericos exauctoratos curiae tradendos et post poenam spiritualem corporaliter puniendos.* Thomas replies that this is contrary to the canons—*Nec enim Deus iudicat bis in idipsum.* He argues that the judgment of the ecclesiastical court must put an end to the whole case. It condemns a clerk to degradation. If that is a correct it must also be a complete judgment. It ought not to be followed by any other sentence.

The story as told by 'Anonymus II.' is to the same effect. The king's demand is thus described:—

ut in clericos publicorum criminum reos de ipsorum [sc. episcoporum] consilio sibi liceret quod avitis diebus factum sua curia recolebat; tales enim deprehensos et convictos aut confessos *mox degradari*, sicque poenis publicis sicut et laicos subdi, tunc usurpatum est.²

To this the bishops reply, not that a lay tribunal is incompetent to try an accused clerk, but *Non iudicabit Deus bis in idipsum.*

Yet more instructive is 'Anonymus I.' The king's officers, instigated by the devil, took to arresting clerks, investigated the charges against them, and, if those charges were found true, committed the accused to gaol. (We must note by the way that even these royal officers, though instigated by the devil, do not condemn clerks to death or mutilation, but merely send them to prison.) The archbishop, however, held that though these men were notoriously guilty, the church ought not to desert them, and he threatened to excommunicate any who should pass judgment upon them elsewhere

[1] *Materials*, iv. 202.   [2] *Ibid.* iv. 96.

than in the ecclesiastical court. Thereupon the king, admitting the reasonableness of this assertion (*necessitate rationis compulsus*), consented that they should be given up to the bishops, upon condition that if they should be degraded by their ecclesiastical superiors they should then be delivered back to the temporal power for condemnation (*ita tamen ut et ipse [archiepiscopus] eos meritis exigentibus exordinatos suis ministris condemnandos traderet*). Thereupon Thomas, as is usual, is ready with the *Nemo bis in idipsum*.[1] This is an instructive account of the matter, because, as I read it, it distinctly represents Henry as not venturing to make the claim which he is commonly supposed to have made. No doubt he would like to try clerks in his court, but he knows that the church will never consent to this.

Testimony that could be put into the other scale I cannot find. True, it is often said that the king wants 'to draw clerks to secular judgments (*trahere clericos ad saecularia iudicia*).' This was Becket's own phrase;[2] and, though I do not think that it was strictly and technically true, I think that in the mouth of a controversialist it was true enough. Henry did propose that clerks should be accused in his court, and he did propose that punishment should be inflicted by the temporal power upon criminals who were clerks when they committed their crimes. The archbishop might from his own point of view represent as a mere sophism the argument that during the preliminary proceedings in the lay court there was no judgment, and that during the final proceedings there was no clerk. But we can hardly set this somewhat vague phrase, 'to draw clerks to secular judgments,' in the balance against the detailed

---

[1] *Materials*, iv. 39.
[2] Letter by Thomas to the pope, *Materials*, v. 388.

accounts of Henry's proposals which we have had from other quarters, in particular against the plain words of Ralph de Diceto.

But we have yet to consider the story told by Herbert of Bosham. He says that the king was advised that his proposed treatment of criminous clerks was in accordance with the canons, and that this advice was given by men who professed themselves learned *in utroque iure*. Herbert sneers at these legists and canonists as being *scienter indocti*; still he admits that they appealed to the text of the canon law. He puts an argument about that text into their mouths, and then proceeds to refute it in the archbishop's name. Now if Henry proposed to try criminous clerks in a temporal forum, he had no case on the Decretum Gratiani, and no one would for one moment have doubted but that he was breaking canon after canon. However, we have Herbert's word for it that the king's advisers thought, or at all events said, that the king's scheme was sanctioned by the law of the church, and with Herbert's help we may yet find in the Corpus Iuris Canonici the words upon which they relied. It will, I suppose, hardly be questioned that Herbert may be trusted about this matter, for he is making an admission against the interest of his hero, St. Thomas; he is admitting that the king's partisans professed themselves willing to stand or fall by the canon law. And the story is corroborated by phrases which are casually used by other writers, phrases to which I have drawn attention by italic type. When Ralph de Diceto writes *curiae traderet puniendos*, when the author of *Summa Causae* writes *curiae meae lictoribus tradantur*, when Anonymus II. writes *mox degradari*, they are one and all alluding to certain phrases in Gratian's book.

The debate, as I understand it, turned on two

passages in the Decretum.¹ One of them is the following :—

> Decr. C. 11, qu. 1, c. 18 : *Clericus suo inobediens episcopo* **depositus** *curiae tradatur.*
>
> *Item Pius Papa epist. ii.*
>
> Si quis sacerdotum **vel** reliquorum clericorum suo episcopo inobediens fuerit, aut ei insidias paraverit, aut contumeliam, **aut** calumniam, vel convicia intulerit, **et** convinci potuerit, mox [depositus ²] curiae tradatur, et recipiat quod inique gessit.

The other of the two is introduced by a *dictum Gratiani* which ends thus :—

> In **criminali** vero causa non nisi ante episcopum clericus examin**andus est.** Et hoc est illud, quod legibus et canonibus supra diffinitum **est,** ut in criminali videlicet causa ante civilem iudicem nullus clericus producatur, **nisi** forte **cum consensu** episcopi **sui; veluti** quando incorrigibiles inveniuntur, tunc detracto eis officio **curiae** tradendi sunt. Unde Fabianus **Papa ait ep. ii. Episcopis orientalibus. . . .**

On this follows Decr. C. 11, qu. 1, c. 31 :—

> *Qui episcopo insidiatur semotus a clero curiae tradatur.*
>
> Statuimus, ut, si quis clericorum suis episcopis infestus aut insidiator extiterit, **mox ante** examinatum iudicium submotus a clero curiae tradatur, cui diebus vitae **suae deserviat, et infamis absque ulla spe restitutionis permaneat.**

These passages, it will be seen, contain more than once the phrase *curiae tradere*. What is the true meaning of it?

This seems to me an almost unanswerable question, for it amounts to this : By what standard shall we, standing in the twelfth century, construe certain passages which we believe to come from two popes, the one of the

---

¹ *Materials*, iii. 266–270.

² It will be seen hereafter that this word is not in the text of the Pseudo-Isidore, nor is it in the *Decretum Ivonis*, p. 5, c. 243.

second, the other of the third century, but which really come from a forger of the ninth, who, it is probable, has been using an imperial constitution of the fifth?

Apparently the disputable phrase takes us back in the last resort to a constitution of Arcadius and Honorius, which was received into the Theodosian code.[1] It begins thus:—

> Quemcunque clericum indignum officio suo episcopus iudicaverit et ab ecclesiae ministerio segregaverit, aut si qui professum sacrae religionis obsequium sponte dereliquerit, continuo eum curia sibi vindicet, ut liber illi ultra ad ecclesiam recursus esse non possit, et pro hominum qualitate et quantitate patrimonii, vel ordini suo vel collegio civitatis adiungatur; modo ut quibuscunque apti erunt publicis necessitatibus obligentur, ita ut colludio quoque locus non sit.

Then having in his mind this text, or rather an epitome of the West Goth's interpretation of this text, the Pseudo-Isidore inserted certain clauses into the decretals that he was concocting for Pope Pius I. and Pope Fabian.[2] What he says in the name of Fabian we need not repeat, for it is fairly enough represented by the second of the two passages that are quoted above from Gratian.[3] What he says in the name of Pius is this:—

> Et si quis sacerdotum vel reliquorum clericorum suo episcopo inobediens fuerit aut ei insidias paraverit aut calumniam et convinci poterit, mox curiae tradatur. Qui autem facit iniuriam, recipiat hoc quod inique gessit.[4]

There is here enough difference between Gratian and Isidore to make us doubt whether the one fully understood the other. But yet a third time did the great

---

[1] Lib. xvi. tit. ii. l. 39.
[2] Hinschius would trace these passages to an epitome of the *Breviarium Alarici*, which is represented by the Paris manuscript, *sup. lat.* 215. See Haenel, *Lex Romana Visigothorum*, pp. 246-248.
[3] Fabianus, xxi. (ed. Hinschius, p. 165).
[4] Pius, x. (Hinschius, p. 120).

forger return to this theme. To the pen of Pope Stephen he ascribed the following words:—

Clericus ergo qui episcopum suum accusaverit aut ei insidiator extiterit, non est recipiendus, quia infamis effectus est et a gradu debet recedere aut curiae tradi serviendus.[1]

Now, of course, the phrase in the Theodosian code, *continuo eum curia sibi vindicet*, has nothing whatever to do with the point at issue between Henry and Becket. The clerk who has been degraded from, or who has renounced, his holy orders is to become a *curialis*; he is to become obnoxious to all those duties and burdens, those *munera*, by which in the last days of the empire the *curiales* were being crushed. I suppose that no words of ours will serve as equivalents for the *curia* and the *curialis* of the fourth and fifth centuries; even German writers, with all their resources, leave these terms untranslated. I suppose that if Henry had wished to substitute for the words of Arcadius and Honorius a phrase which would express their meaning, and be thoroughly intelligible to his English subjects, he would have said: *Clericus degradatus debet scottare et lottare cum laicis*. It would seem also that Becket and his canonists knew something of the history of the words *tradatur curiae*, and were prepared to go behind Gratian. But what I am concerned to point out is that on the text of the Decretum Henry had an arguable case. Here, he might say, are words that are plain enough. A clerk disobeys or insults his bishop; *mox depositus curiae tradatur, et recipiat quod inique gessit*. What can this mean if it be not that the offender, having been deposed by his bishop, is to be handed over to the *curia*, the lay court, for further punishment? Very well, that is what I am contending for. Further punishment after

[1] Stephanus, xii. (Hinschius, p. 186).

degradation does not infringe your sacred maxim *Nemo bis in idipsum*, or, if it does, then you are prepared to infringe that maxim yourselves whenever to do so will serve your turn.

But more than this can be said. Not very long after Henry's death the greatest of all the popes put an interpretation on the phrase *curiae tradere*. Innocent III. issued a constitution against the forgers of papal letters. The forgers, if they are clerks, are to be degraded, and then

postquam per ecclesiasticum iudicem fuerint degradati, saeculari potestati tradantur secundum constitutiones legitimas puniendi, per quam et laici, qui fuerint de falsitate convicti, legitime puniantur [c. 7, X. 5. 20].[1]

This seems plain enough. Henry, had he been endowed with the gift of prophecy, might have said: 'Here, at any rate, is an exception to your principle, and for my own part I cannot see that the forgery of a decretal—though I will admit, if you wish it, that it is wicked to forge decretals—is a much worse crime than murder, or rape, or robbery.'

But this is nothing to what follows. Innocent III. speaks once more (c. 27, X. 5. 40):[2]—

Novimus expedire ut verbum illud quod et in antiquis canonibus, et in nostro quoque decreto contra falsarios edito continetur, videlicet ut clericus, per ecclesiasticum iudicem degradatus, saeculari tradatur curiae puniendus, apertius exponamus. Quum enim quidam antecessorum nostrorum, super hoc consulti, diversa responderint, et quorundam sit opinio a pluribus approbata, ut clericus qui propter hoc vel aliud flagitium grave, non solum damnabile, sed damnosum, fuerit degradatus, tanquam exutus privilegio clericali saeculari foro per consequentiam applicetur, quum ab ecclesiastico foro fuerit proiectus ; eius est degradatio celebranda saeculari potestate praesente, ac pronunciandum est eidem, quum fuerit celebrata, ut in suum forum recipiat degradatum, et sic intelligitur 'tradi curiae saeculari'; pro quo tamen debet ecclesia efficaciter intercedere, ut citra mortis periculum circa eum sententia moderetur.

---

[1] *Reg. Inn. III.*, ed. Baluze, i. 574.   [2] *Ibid.* ii. 268.

Now this, as I understand it, is an authoritative exposition of the true intent and meaning of the phrase *tradere curiae* contained in those passages from the Decretum which have been printed above. It was a dubious phrase; some read it one way, some another; but on the whole the better opinion is not that of St. Thomas, but that of King Henry. And so the king's advisers have this answer to the sneers of Master Herbert of Bosham:—We cannot hope to be better canonists than Pope Innocent III. will be.

I am not arguing that Henry's scheme ought to have satisfied those who took their stand on the Decretum. From their point of view the preliminary procedure in the king's court, whereby the civil magistrate acquired a control over the case, would be objectionable, and the mission of royal officers to watch the trial in the spiritual court might be offensive. But still about the main question that was in debate, the question of double punishment, Henry had something to say, and something which the highest of high churchmen could not refuse to hear.

This account of the matter seems to fit in with all that we know of the behaviour of Alexander III. and of the English bishops. Had Henry been striving to subject criminous clerks to the judgment of the temporal forum, the case against him would have been exceedingly plain. A pope, however much beset by troubles, could hardly have hesitated about it; no bishop could have taken the king's side without openly repudiating what passed as the written law of the church. But the pope hesitated, and the English bishops, to say the least, did not stubbornly resist the king's proposal. Even Becket's own conduct seems best explained by the supposition that until he grew warm with controversy he was not very certain of the ground that he had to defend.

10

Mox depositus curiae tradatur et recipiat quod inique gessit was ringing in one ear: *Nec enim Deus iudicat bis in idipsum* in the other ear.

If, then, we were to found our judgment only on the purely English evidence, upon the words of the debated article, and upon the stories that are told by chroniclers and biographers, we should have good reason for holding that Henry II. did not demand that a clerk accused of crime should be tried by a temporal court. I believe that a little research among foreign books would strengthen us in our conviction, by showing that the scheme which I have attributed to him, the scheme which sends the clerk to and fro between the royal judge and the bishop, had for a long time past been a well-known arrangement, and was one that Henry was likely to regard as ancient and legitimate.[1] Indeed, if I am right about the meaning of the article, then the struggle between the English king and the English prelate will neatly fall into its proper place in the general history of church and state. The dispute will be over a fairly disputable question, though perhaps we shall come to the conclusion that Becket rather than Henry was the innovator.[2] On the other hand, if Henry attempts to abolish the *privilegium fori*, he is to my mind incredibly before or behind his age.

I must admit, however, that many things which seem incredible to me have seemed credible to honoured historians of the English church. I will give one example. In Dr. Hook's *Lives of the Archbishops of Canterbury* I find the following words:[3]—'Bracton, indeed, who was made a judge by Henry III. in the

---

[1] Hinschius, *Kirchenrecht*, iv. 794 ff., 849 ff., v. 402 ff.

[2] Of this something has been said elsewhere, *History of English Law*, i. 432.

[3] *Lives of the Archbishops* (1872), vol. ix. (Parker) p. 166, footnote.

thirteenth century, when **popery was** rampant, expresses himself thus *Rex est vicarius et minister Dei, tam in spiritualibus quam in temporalibus*, Lib. i. cap. 8.' I wish that I could believe Dr. Hook's statement, for, were it true, Bracton would be by far the most remarkable man of his time. However, what Bracton wrote in 'Lib. i. cap. 8' was much more commonplace and papistical: '*Apud homines vero est differentia personarum, quia hominum quidam sunt precellentes et prelati et aliis principantur: dominus papa videlicet in rebus spiritualibus, quae pertinent ad sacerdotium, et sub eo archiepiscopi, episcopi et alii prelati inferiores: item in temporalibus sunt imperatores, reges et principes, in hiis quae pertinent ad regnum.*' Where Dr. Hook found the words that he quotes I do not know. Protestant lawyers of the sixteenth century sometimes wrote funny things in the margins of their Bractons, and Coke sometimes took Bracton's name in vain. But as to Bracton himself, though he was for his time a strong opponent of the extremer claims of the ecclesiastical party, he never said that the king was God's vicar in spiritual matters. And even so it is in the case of Henry II. Whatever he may have wished, I cannot believe that he had any hope of securing the consent of the English bishops to a treatment of accused clerks which was unquestionably condemned by the Decretum.

V. 'EXECRABILIS' IN THE COMMON PLEAS

Towards the middle of Edward III.'s reign, just when a national resistance against papal 'provisors' was being organised, the king's legal advisers and the justices of the court of Common Pleas took upon themselves to enforce a certain papal constitution, though to enforce it in an odd, lopsided fashion, favourable to their royal lord. The pope's weapons were to be wrested from his hand and used against him. The king was going to exercise ecclesiastical patronage which the pope had destined for himself. This clever move is partially revealed to us by certain discussions in the Year Books, which have never, I believe, been fully explained because they have never been compared with the plea rolls. The story may be worth telling.

The constitution in question was none other than the famous *Execrabilis*, which fills a prominent place in the constitutional history of the catholic church. It is one of the stock examples of those covetously fiscal 'extravagants' which are characteristic of the Avignonese papacy. Perhaps we remember how Rabelais speaks of 'the terrific chapters, *Execrabilis, De multa, Si plures* . . . and certain others, which draw every year four hundred thousand ducats and more from France to Rome.'[1] For some time past popes and councils had

[1] *Works of Rabelais*, transl. W. F. Smith, ii. 217.

been legislating against pluralism: that is, against the simultaneous tenure by one clerk of more than one benefice involving a cure of souls.[1] Among the laws striking at this evil was a canon of the fourth Lateran Council (1215), which began with the words *De multa*.[2] This canon is here mentioned merely because a tradition among English lawyers taught, and perhaps still teaches, that a reference was made to it in the cases which are to come before us; but we shall hereafter see that this tradition has its origin in a mistake. Legislation, however, was futile. The popes themselves made it futile by their dispensations, and those who do not like popes tell us that the laws were made in order that they might be dispensed with. At last, in November 1317, John XXII. issued a long and stringent constitution whose first word was *Execrabilis*.[3] It was stringent; it was retrospective; it attacked those clerks who were already holding several 'incompatible' benefices; it attacked them even though they had obtained dispensations. Such a clerk was, within one month after notice of this constitution, to resign all but one of his benefices, or else they were all to be vacant *ipso iure*. There were prospective besides retrospective clauses, and finally there was a clause in which we may, if we like, discover the legislator's main motive. All the benefices vacated by the 'cession' of the pluralists were 'reserved' to the pope, or, in other words, it was for him to fill the vacancies. This constitution was no idle word in England. In the next year we can see Pope John busily at work collating clerks to English benefices which have been vacated by the force of *Execrabilis*.[4] The English

---

[1] For a full historical account of the law see Hinschius, Kirchenrecht, III. 243 ff.

[2] Conc. Lat. IV. c. 29; c. 28, X. 3. 5.

[3] c. un. in Extrav. Joan. XXII. 3; c. 4 in Extrav. comm. 3. 2.

[4] *Calendar of Papal Letters*, II. 172–182.

king was weak and worthless, and apparently the Holy Father was allowed to have his way.

A little later Edward III. was on the throne, and the outcry against 'provisors' was swelling. At this moment some of the king's lawyers seem to have caught at the idea that two could play at *Execrabilis*, and that, while the 'reservation' was studiously disregarded, the main provisions of the bull might be enforced with advantage. It will be remembered that the amount of patronage that fell to the king's share was very large. To say nothing of the churches that were all his own, he exercised the patronage of infants who were in ward to him, and also the patronage annexed to bishoprics that were vacant. So any measure which emptied churches might do him a good turn and enable him to pay his servants.

In 1335 the king brought a *Quare impedit* against the bishop of Norwich for the deanery of Lynn.[1] The king stated in his count that John, late bishop of Norwich [that is, John Salmon who died in 1325], had conferred the deanery on one Master Roger of Snettisham, who was already parson of the church of Cressingham, and who continued to hold both benefices for more than a month after his installation in the deanery, 'per quod per constitucionem de pluralite predictus decanatus vacavit ipso iure,' and remained vacant until the temporalities of the bishopric of Norwich came into the hand of Edward II. upon the death of bishop John. To this declaration the bishop demurred in that polite form in which we demur to the pleadings of kings. He said that he did not understand that the king desired an answer to the said declaration, 'for therein he does not

---

[1] De Banco Roll, No. 305, Hilary to Edw. III. m. 214 dors. An earlier stage on De Banco Roll, No. 303, Trinity 9 Edw. III. m. 236. I have to thank Miss Salisbury for extracts from these rolls.

allege that the said deanery was vacant *de facto* in such wise that this court might take cognisance of the vacancy, but merely alleges that it was vacant by the constitution against plurality, which does not fall within the cognisance of this court.' So the bishop craved judgment. The king replied that by the constitution against plurality the deanery must be adjudged to have been vacant *de iure* just as though the dean had been deprived thereof by sentence. So the king craved judgment. Here the record ends, and no more of the case has been found.

So much from the roll. In the Year Book we have discussion.[1] After some little fencing over the question whether the king ought to say that a 'bishopric' is (or merely that the 'temporalities of a bishopric' are) in his hand when there is no bishop, the serjeants come to the main matter. For the bishop it is said: 'Sir, you see how the king takes as the cause of the voidance the constitution touching plurality, and shows nothing that lies in any fact which would give cognisance to this court, such as resignation, privation, death or succession.' Parning, who is arguing for the king, replies: 'The constitution touching plurality was made by a general judgment that all should be deprived who held their *beneficia curata* for more than a month after the constitution, and this binds them more firmly as regards privation than a judgment that some certain person should be deprived, for the one might be afterwards annulled upon appeal; not so the other.'

The Year Book, like the roll, tells of no judgment. Probably the king and the bishop came to terms. We can, I think, see that the king's advocates were steering a difficult course. They were proposing to enforce a papal constitution directly and without any certificate from the

[1] Y. B. 9 Edw. III. f. 22 (Trin. pl. 14 ; Y. B. 10 Edw. III. f. 42 (Hil. pl. 3).

English ordinary. What might they not have on their hands if they once began to administer the 'extravagants' of Avignon? Parning's argument seems to be explicable by the retrospective character of *Execrabilis*. This, he urges, is a 'general judgment.' If a particular judgment of deprivation were given against a clerk and were certified to this court, you would hold that the benefice was vacant. Well, here is a general judgment and one that is subject to no appeal. That the constitution in question was *Execrabilis* and not one of the earlier decrees (for example, *De multa*), would, I believe, be clear even from this case, because of the mention made of the one month which is given to the pluralist for the resignation of his superabundant benefices. Happily, however, this is put beyond all doubt by the enrolled record of the next case, though it is left dubious in the Year Book.

In 1351, John of Gaunt, on behalf of the king, brought a *Quod permittat* against Simon Islip, archbishop of Canterbury, for a presentation to the church of Wimbledon in the county of Surrey.[1] The king's declaration stated that Robert of Winchelsea, archbishop of Canterbury, being seised of the advowson, collated John of Sandale in the eleventh year of the reign of Edward II., and that because Pope John, in the second year of his pontificate (Sept. 5, 1317–1318) and the ninth year of the said reign (July 8, 1315–1316),[2] made a certain constitution called *Execrabilis*, to the effect that no clerk should occupy two *beneficia curata* beyond one month after the publication of the said constitution without being deprived *ipso iure* of both benefices, which constitution was published in the said year of Edward II., and because the said John of Sandale occupied the

[1] De Banco Roll, Mich. 25 Edw. III. m. 41 dors.
[2] The slight discrepancy in the dates will be noticed.

church of Wimbledon and various other churches [which are named] for days and years after the said publication, the said church of Wimbledon by virtue of the said constitution became vacant, and remained vacant until the temporalities of the archbishopric came into Edward II.'s hands by the death of archbishop Robert, and so the right to present a clerk pertained to Edward II., from whom it descended to the now king.

Pausing here for a moment, we may remark that to us who are blessed with books of reference, the king's story is obviously false, for Robert Winchelsea was dead, and Walter Reynolds had succeeded him at Canterbury some time before the publication of *Execrabilis*. But we must not allow this brutal matter of fact to spoil matter of law. We learn from the Year Book[1] that the counsel for the archbishop were at first inclined to demur. The king, they said, founds his action on a matter that does not lie in the cognisance of this court, and we do not think that this court will take cognisance of a matter which ought to be pleaded in court Christian. This was an intelligible line of defence : it is not for the court of Common Pleas to enforce directly a law against plurality. However, we are told that the archbishop's counsel dared not demur at this point, since if the court was against them they would be allowed no other defence. So they, as both the report and the record show, traversed the king's statement that the church of Wimbledon fell vacant while the temporalities of the archbishopric were in the hands of Edward II. This is the plea that is upon the roll, where no notice is taken of the abortive demurrer. A jury was summoned and gave the king a verdict. The jurors said upon their oath that after the publication in England of the constitution called *Execrabilis*, for some six weeks and

[1] Y. B. 26 Edw. III. f. 1 (Pasch. pl. 3).

more, John of Sandale held the church of Wimbledon and certain other churches which they named, that thereby the said church became vacant, and that it remained vacant until by the death of archbishop Robert the temporalities of the archbishopric came into the hands of Edward II. Judgment was given that the king should recover his presentation, and that the archbishop was in mercy.[1]

On the roll this judgment is followed by a remarkable writ, dated April 22, 1352. Much to our surprise the king confesses that he is now informed that the title to the presentation which he had successfully urged was feigned and untrue (*fictus et non verus*), and that the church did not become vacant while the temporalities of the archbishopric were in his father's hand. Therefore he revokes his presentation of a certain William of Cheston, declares that the judgment is not to be enforced, and forbids that the archbishop should be further molested. This writ comes to us as a surprise; for though, as already said, we happen to know that the jurors' verdict must have been false when it supposed that Winchelsea's death occurred after the publication of Pope John's constitution, still we are hardly prepared to see Edward III. quietly resigning the fruits of a judgment. The interesting feature of the case, however, is the proof that the court of Common Pleas was prepared to put in force one half of the notorious extravagant, and this without requiring any sentence of deprivation pronounced by an English ecclesiastical court. The pope had said that in a certain event a benefice was to be void; void therefore it was, for the pope had power to make laws and even retrospective laws against plur-

---

[1] See also the case against the bishop of Worcester, Y. B. 24 Edw. III. f. 29 Trin. pl. 21; also the earlier cases Y. B. 14 15 Edw. III. (ed. Pike) 36, 70; 15 Edw. III. ed. Pike, 163.

alism. On the other hand, no word is said in record or report of the other half of the bull, for a 'reservation' is plainly an attempt to touch that right of patronage which is a temporal right given by the law of the land, and such an attempt is *ultra vires statuentis*. The pope's law may turn an incumbent out, but, the church being vacant, the patron can exercise his right of presentation. A very pretty plan! But what would **the** English prelates say?

We can now understand a petition that the clergy presented to the king in the Parliament of 1351.[1] Probably it was occasioned by the action directed against the archbishop. 'May it please you to grant that henceforth no justice shall hold plea of the vacation of any benefice of Holy Church by reason of insufficient age, consecration as bishop, resignation, plurality, inability, or other voidance *de* **iure, for no** such avoidance lies or can **be in the cognisance of lay folk ; but if** our lord the king desires **to take** advantage **of** any **such** avoidance *de iure*, let a mandate be sent to the archbishop or bishop of the place where the benefice **is,** bidding him inquire touching this matter in the due manner according to the law of Holy Church as is done in the case of bastardy.' In answer to this prayer the king willed that if title by avoidance came in plea before his justices, whereof the cognisance appertained **to** court Christian, the party[2] should have his challenge, **and the** justices should do right. This somewhat enigmatical response **was converted** into a statute.[3] 'Whereas the said prelates have prayed remedy **because** the secular justices accroach to themselves cognisance of the vacation **of** benefices, whereof the cognisance and discussion belongs to the

---

[1] *Rolls of Parliament*, ii. 245.
[2] The statute suggests that **the word should** be *prelate* not *party*.
[3] 25 Edw. III. stat. 3, **cap. 8.**

judge of Holy Church and not to the lay judge, the king wills that the justices shall henceforth receive the challenges made or to be made by any prelates of Holy Church in this behalf, and shall do right and reason in respect of the same.' This statute, like many others which touch the relation of the temporal to the spiritual tribunals, looks very much like an 'As you were.' Bishops and justices must fight the matter out: both parties should be reasonable; but the king does not like to decide their quarrels.

I believe that the justices held their ground. The traditional law of Coke's day was that 'by the constitution of the pope' if a clergyman accepts a second benefice 'the first is void *ipso iure* and the patron may present if he will,' although no sentence of deprivation has been passed.[1] In other words, the secular court would take direct notice of the ecclesiastical rule which avoids the one *beneficium curatum* when the other is accepted. Coke thought that the rule in question was the outcome of *De multa*, the canon of the Lateran Council of 1215. That canon would, in fact, have sanctioned what was done by our courts of common law; but when Coke proceeds to say that this is the constitution that is referred to in the cases of Edward III.'s day, he is mistaken. He had seen the Year Books, but did not know that the roll spoke expressly of Pope John and his *Execrabilis*.

Having mentioned John of Sandale and pluralism, it may be worth our while to observe that a clerk of this name, while working his way upwards through the king's service towards the chancellorship of the realm and the bishopric of Winchester, became a pluralist of the deepest dye. He, when yet a subdeacon, obtained the chancellorship of St. Patrick's at

---

[1] *Holland's* case, 4 Rep. 75*a*; *Digby's* case, 4 Rep. 78*b*.

Dublin, the treasurership of Lichfield, seven churches in seven dioceses, and three prebends at Wells, Howden, and Beverley, and had leave from the pope to accept additional benefices to the value of £200.¹ The requisite dispensation he had obtained from Clement v. at the instance of the king of England. This is a good illustration of that viciously circular process from which an escape was impossible until the pope's claims were utterly denied. The king's 'civil service' must be maintained, but can only be maintained out of the revenues of the churches, such is the people's impatience of taxation. The only method, however, by which these revenues can be secured for such an object must be found in papal dispensations. Therefore the pope's power to dispense with the laws that he has ordained must be acknowledged. And then when the pope tries to make profit for himself out of the power that we allow to him, we begin to complain and to pass 'statutes of provisors,' which we dare not enforce lest the king's 'civil service' should break down. We cannot get on with the pope, and yet we cannot do without him, for rightly or wrongly we think that he can legislate for the church. If only we could say that his laws are not binding on a national church which has not accepted them! We dare not say that; we do not believe it; such independence as our national church enjoys is secured for it by the blessed, if uncanonical, principle that an advowson is temporal property. In the nineteenth century that principle may be out of date and deserve to be whittled away; but Anglicans should speak well of the bridge that carried them over the flood of Extravagants.

¹ *Register of Papal Letters*, ii. 9, 27, 88, 119.

VI. THE DEACON AND THE JEWESS

IN the year 1222, Archbishop Stephen Langton held at Oxford a provincial council, and of this council one result was that a deacon was burnt, burnt because he had turned Jew for the love of a Jewess.

I propose here to set in order the scattered evidence that we have for this story. This, so far as I am aware, has not yet been done, and it seems worth doing. The story became famous, for the passage in which Bracton made mention of it became the main, almost the only, support for the statement that English common (that is, non-statutory) law can and will burn a heretic. We have indeed no warrant for saying that from the death of this deacon until the death of Sautre in 1401 no one in England was burnt for heresy, but we may say with some confidence that during this long period, near two hundred years, if English orthodoxy had a victim, there is no known record of his fate.[1]

Now for just so much of the tale as is told above we have testimony ample in quantity and excellent in quality. But I have purposely used a loose phrase :— the apostate's death was a 'result' of the council. If we strive to be more precise and ask by what authority he was committed to the flames, who passed, who executed the sentence, we have before us a difficult problem. Not only in course of time did the solid

[1] *Report of Ecclesiastical Courts Commission*, 1883, *Historical Appendix*, p. 52.

tragic fact attract to itself some floating waifs of legend and miracle, but even our best witnesses have not been so careful of their words as doubtless they would have been had they known that they were writing for an ignorant nineteenth century. We must collate their testimonies, mark what they say, also what they do not say. So doing we shall be drawn into noticing another story about a man and a woman who were immured (whatever 'immured' may mean), and this story also deserves being brought to light, for it is curious.

That the council was held is certain. The scene and time we can fix. The scene was Oxford, or, to be more particular, the conventual church of Oseney.[1] The day is variously described: the day on which we read in the gospel, 'I am the good Shepherd,' the day on which we sing in the introit, 'The earth is full of the mercy of the Lord'; but all descriptions come to this, it was the 17th of April, and the Second Sunday after Easter, in the year 1222. The canons which the council published we have.[2] Naturally enough, being general ordinances, they say nothing of the deacon; but there are two of them which claim a brief attention.

It was ordained that no beneficed clerk, or clerk in holy orders, should take any part whatever, even the most mechanical and subordinate, in the judicial shedding of blood.[3] This, even if it stood by itself, would assure us that no sentence of death was pronounced by the council in so many words. It may be that this canon was habitually disobeyed, or obeyed only according to its very letter. At this time, and for some years afterwards, many of the judges in our king's court (to say

[1] *Annales Monastici* (Oseney), vol. iv. p. 62.
[2] Wilkins, *Concilia*, vol. i. p. 585.   [3] Cap. 7.

nothing of bishops, and even abbots sent out as justices in eyre) were ecclesiastics, and the judicial bench was often a step to the episcopal throne. But this was a scandal to churchmen of the straiter sort, and it would be one thing for a beneficed clerk to hold pleas of the crown, leaving to some lay associate the actual uttering of the fatal *suspendatur*, quite another for an ecclesiastical council to break while in the act of publishing a law for the church.

Also the council had something to say about the mingling of Jews with Christians, and something which suggests, what indeed seems the truth, that at this time the Jews in England, despite the exactions of their royal protector, and despite occasional outbursts of popular fury, were a prosperous thriving race. Jews are not to have Christian servants, it being contrary to reason that the sons of the free woman should serve the sons of the bond.[1] Again, there being unfortunately no visible distinction between Jews and Christians, there have been mixed marriages or less permanent unions; for the better prevention whereof, it is ordained that every Jew shall wear on the front of his dress tablets or patches of cloth four inches long by two wide, of some colour other than that of the rest of his garment.[2] We might guess that the prelates were moved to this decree by the then recent and shameful crime of the apostate deacon. But there is no need for any such supposition, for the Oxford Council was publishing and endorsing the acts of a more august assembly, the fourth Lateran Council held by Pope Innocent III. in the year 1215.

[1] Cap. 39.
[2] Cap. 40. It seems that this regulation was enforced by statute in 1275. See *Flores Historiarum* ('Matthew of Westminster') for that year. In *Statutes of the Realm* (vol. i. p. 221) this appears as a statute of uncertain date.

The Lateran Council had prohibited the clergy from taking part in judgment of blood,¹ also it had ordained that Jews and Saracens should wear some distinctive garb,² lest under cover of a mistake there should be an unholy union of those whom God had put asunder. But this was by-work; the suppression of flagrant heresy had been the main matter in hand. Of heresy England had known little, almost nothing. It is true that in 1166 some heretics, Cathari or the like, had been condemned by an ecclesiastical council (this council also was held at Oxford), had been handed over to the secular power, and then by the king's command whipt, branded, and exiled; some of them, it seems, miserably perished of cold and hunger.³ But they were foreigners, and the writer who tells us most about them boasts that though Britain was disgraced by the birth of Pelagius, England, since it had become England, had been unpolluted by false doctrine. He boasts also, and apparently with truth, that well-timed severity had been successful.⁴ Only one other case is recorded, and of this we know next to nothing. In 1210 an Albigensian was burnt in London; we are told just this and no more.⁵ It must not surprise us, therefore, if English law had no well-settled procedure for cases of heresy; there had been no heretics. But it was otherwise elsewhere. When the Lateran Council met, the Albigensian war had been raging, and it had been a serious question whether a large tract of France would not be permanently lost to the catholic church. So one great object of the council was to impress upon all princes and

¹ Cap. 18. ² Cap. 68.
³ The original authorities seem to be Rad. de Diceto ed. Stubbs, vol. i. p. 318; William of Newburgh (ed. Howlett), vol. i. p. 131; Mapes de Nugis Curialium, p. 63; Ralph of Coggeshall, p. 122.
⁴ Will. Newburgh, l.c.
⁵ *Liber de Antiquis Legibus* (Camden Society), p. 3.

11

potentates the sacred duty of extirpating heretics. A definite method of dealing with them was ordained.¹ They were to be condemned by the ecclesiastical powers in the presence of the secular powers or their bailiffs (*saecularibus potestatibus praesentibus aut eorum baillivis*) and delivered to due punishment, clerks being first deprived of their orders. Also it was decreed that if the temporal lord, when required and admonished by the church, neglected to purge his land of heresy, he should be excommunicated by the metropolitan and the other bishops of the province. If, then, for the space of a year he should still be contumacious, that was to be signified to the pope, who would thereupon discharge the subjects of this recalcitrant prince from their allegiance. The due punishment for the obstinate heretic was not defined. By this time so many had suffered it that there was little need to name it, and it was one that ecclesiastical councils scrupled to name. From taking part in such legislation as this the English bishops had lately returned when they met at Oxford. The council at Oxford, having recited and republished the Lateran canons, can have had little doubt as to how it and the secular powers ought to deal with a deacon who had turned Jew.

It will hardly be a digression, and indeed may lead us to the right point of view, if we notice that this same Lateran Council made (or if the word *made* be objectionable, then let us say *caused*) a great change in English criminal law. It abolished the ordeal, or rather it made the ordeal impossible by forbidding the clergy to take part in the ceremony.² No more remained for the council of the English king (the king himself was yet a boy) than to find some substitute for a procedure which was no longer practicable.³ We may respect the motives

---

¹ Cap. 3. This is c. 13, X. 5. 7.   ² Cap. 18.
³ See the orders issued to the justices in eyre; *Foedera*, vol. i. p. 154.

which urged Blackstone to protest that no change in English law could be made by a body of prelates assembled at Rome;[1] but we shall misread the history of the time unless we understand that the exclusive power of the church to rule things spiritual—and the ordeal, the judgment of God, was a thing spiritual—was unquestioned. And so also in the matter of heresy it was for the church to speak, and her speech might end with an eloquent aposiopesis.

Though it may delay us from our story, there is yet one question which should be asked and answered before we can fully comprehend the evidence that is to come before us. Who at Oxford in the year 1222 was the natural and proper representative of temporal power: who was the *manus laicalis*? Doubtless the sheriff of Oxfordshire. Now it happened that the sheriff of Oxfordshire was one of the most important men in England: more than king in England (*plusquam rex in Anglia*), some said.[2] He was Fawkes of Bréauté, just at the full height of his power, a man not unlikely to act in a high-handed imperious way without much regard for forms and precedents, a man who perhaps was already plotting revolt and civil war, a man somewhat given to disseising and otherwise pillaging the clergy, and therefore, it may be, not unwilling to do the church a service if that service would cost him nothing. He was soon to find that the church could be a terrible enemy, and that of all his foes Langton was the most resolute.

These things premised, we may call the witnesses, and first of all Bracton, not that his testimony is the earliest, but because it is the best known. A lawyer writing for lawyers, he would be likely to see the case in its legal bearings and to speak of it carefully. We

---

[1] *Comment.*, vol. iv. pp. 344, 345.
[2] *Ann. Monast.* Tewkesbury, p. 64.

cannot assign a precise date to his evidence, and he may have given it between thirty and forty years after the event. Still it is from round about the year 1222, the year of the Oxford Council, that he collected most of his case law. That was the time when there were great judges whose judgments were worthy of record. Of their successors, his own contemporaries, he seems for some reason or another to have thought meanly. It was to the examination of old judgments, as he expressly says, that he had given his mind.[1] He is speaking then, if not of his own time, yet of a time that he has studied. He has been telling us that a clerk convicted of crime is to be degraded by the court Christian.[2] This degraded man is to undergo no further punishment; degradation is punishment enough; 'unless indeed he is convicted of apostasy, for then he is to be first degraded and then burnt by the lay power (*per manum laicalem*), as happened at the Oxford Council holden by Stephen, archbishop of Canterbury, of happy memory, touching a deacon who apostatised for a Jewess, and who, when he had been degraded by the bishop, was at once (*statim*) delivered to the fire by the lay power.' Two things we remark. In the first place, there is no talk of any sentence of death being pronounced by any court, temporal or spiritual; there is no talk of any royal writ; the miscreant was burnt at once, on the spot, so soon as he had been degraded: secondly, the case is good law; it is a precedent to be followed when occasion shall require.

But Bracton does not stand alone. If he did, we should perhaps have some cause for doubting his testimony. It was an age fertile of chroniclers, and there are some dozen books in which we may hope to find a trustworthy and early, if not quite contemporary, account

[1] Bracton, f. 1. [2] Bracton, f. 123 b.

of an event which took place in 1222, an event which, though neither very marvellous nor of first-rate importance, was picturesque and unprecedented. Some of these books are silent. The silence most to be regretted is that of Roger of Wendover. We would gladly have had an account from one so careful and so well-informed. But he is busy with more momentous matters, the loss of Damietta and a serious riot in London, not suppressed without the aid of Fawkes and his soldiery. Beyond this he tells of nothing but tempests. And, indeed, the weather this year was bad; about this all our authorities are agreed. It is the only fact that the annalist of Margan found worthy of remark. The annals of Burton and of Bermondsey do not mention the council; those of Winchester Worcester, and Tewkesbury tell us that the council was held, but tell us no more. The annals of Oseney, to which we look hopefully, merely say that the council was held, and held at Oseney. But this silence cannot be reckoned as negative evidence. The monastic annalist, working with no definite plan, with no consistent measure for the greatness of events, jotted down what might interest his house or had struck his fancy, making sometimes what seems to us a capricious selection of facts. He could pass by the fate of the perverted deacon, but he could pass by many things which, tried by any test, were better worth recording.

From the Cistercian house of Waverley in Surrey we have this:[1] 'In this council an apostate deacon who had married (*duxerat*) a Jewess was degraded and afterwards burnt. Also a countryman (*rusticus*) who had crucified himself was immured for ever.' A somewhat longer version comes from Dunstable,[2] and it seems to be the version of one who probably was an eye-witness, Prior Richard Morins, who was describing

---

[1] *Ann. Monast.* vol. ii. p. 296.   [2] *Ibid.* vol. iii. p. 76.

events as they happened year by year. He had certainly been at the Lateran Council, and I suppose that it was his duty to be at the Oxford Council also. He must have been a careful man of business, for these Dunstable Annals are a long detailed record of litigation and legal transactions described in technical language. What he says is this: 'In this council there was condemned to the flames, after his degradation, a deacon who for the love of a Jewess had been circumcised; and he was burnt with fire outside the town by the king's bailiffs who were present on the spot (*ibidem praesentes*). There also another deacon was degraded for theft. Also a woman who gave herself out to be Saint Mary, and a youth who had given himself out to be Christ, and had pierced his own hands, side, and feet, were immured at Banbury.' The prior certainly says that the pervert was condemned to the flames in (not *by*) the council. Could we now draw his attention to these words he would, I think, say (after a grumble about hypercriticism) that, of course, the council did not in so many words pronounce a sentence of death, but would add that it did what was for practical purposes the same thing: it convicted the man of apostasy, and handed him over to the secular power. He might add, too, that no one for whom he wrote would have imagined that a *iudicium sanguinis* was uttered by this assembly of ecclesiastics. Of any temporal court he says nothing, and nothing of any royal writ, but the king's bailiffs were present on the spot, as required by the Lateran Council, and they burnt the convict.

The account which comes to us from the Abbey of Coggeshall in Essex is yet fuller.[1] It is contained in a valuable chronicle, and in all probability was written within some five years after the event. Archbishop

[1] *Ralph of Coggeshall*, p. 190.

Stephen held a council at Oxford, and there 'degraded an apostate deacon, who for the love of a Jewess had circumcised himself. When he had been degraded he was burnt by the servants of the lord Fawkes. And there was brought thither into the council a miscreant youth along with two women, whom the archdeacon of the district accused of the most criminal unbelief, namely, that the youth would not enter a church nor be present at the blessed sacraments, nor obey the injunctions of the Catholic Father, but had suffered himself to be crucified, and still bearing in his body the marks of the wounds, had been pleased to have himself called Jesus by the aforesaid women. And one of the women, an old woman, was accused of having long been given to incantations, and having by her magic arts brought the aforesaid youth to this height of madness. So both being convicted of this gross crime, were condemned to be imprisoned between two walls until they died (*iussi sunt inter duos muros incarcerari quousque deficerent*). But the other woman, who was the youth's sister, was let go free, for she had revealed the impious deed.' We notice the appearance of Fawkes of Bréauté, or rather of his underlings, remembering, however, that the *ministri domini Falconis* would also be the *ballivi domini Regis* mentioned by the prior of Dunstable. We notice also that here there is no sentence of death, and there is no royal writ.

Of about equal value and of about even date must be the account which, according to Dr. Stubbs, comes from some nameless canon of Barnwell: the account which is preserved in the *Memoriale* of Walter of Coventry.[1] 'A priest and a deacon were there degraded inside the church before the council by the lord of Canterbury, the priest for homicide, the deacon for sacrilege and

[1] *Walter of Coventry*, ii. 251.

theft. But another deacon had sinned enormously; he had renounced the Christian faith; blaspheming and apostatising, he had caused himself to be circumcised in imitation of the Jewish rite. He was degraded by the lord of Canterbury outside the church and before the people. Relinquished by the clergy, he was as a layman and captured apostate delivered over to be condemned by the judgment of the lay court, and being at once (*statim*) delivered to the flames he died a miserable death. In degrading the priest and the deacons, when the lord of Canterbury had stripped off the chasuble, or stole, or whatever it might be, by lifting it with the end of his pastoral staff, he made use of these words, "We deprive you of authority" (*Exautoramus te*). There was brought into the council a layman who had allowed himself to be crucified, and the scarred traces of the wounds might be seen in his hands and feet, and his pierced side and his head. There was brought also a woman who, rejecting her own name, had caused herself to be called Mary Mother of Christ. She had given out that she could celebrate mass, and this was manifested by some proofs which were found, for she had made a chalice and patten of wax for the purpose. On these two the council inflicted condign punishment, that enclosed within stone walls (*muris lapideis inclusi*) they should there end life.' One peculiarity of this lifelike account is that it says nothing about the Jewess. But we have also to note the mention of the lay court, for of this we have hitherto heard nothing. The deacon was delivered over to be condemned by its judgment. These are the important words: *velut laicus et apostata captus traditur iudicio curiae laicalis condemnandus*. Nevertheless we do not read that he was in fact condemned by or brought before any secular tribunal; on the contrary, he was forthwith committed to the flames.

I believe that I have now stated what may be called the first-rate evidence, and that it is more than sufficient to establish the chief facts. It will not escape the reader's notice that all these early accounts of the matter are sober: strikingly sober when the nature of the story and its subsequent fate are considered. We come to witnesses of a less trustworthy kind. And first there is Matthew Paris, who died in 1259. Roger of Wendover, as already said, does not mention the Oxford Council. When Paris was absorbing Wendover's work into his own *Chronica Maiora*, he inserted a notice of the council and of the deacon's death. A more elaborate tale he set forth in his *Historia Minor* or *Historia Anglorum*, and to this we will turn first since there he cites his authority, and this authority an eye-witness, one Master John of Basingstoke, archdeacon of London.[1] Of any such archdeacon of London nothing seems known, but a John of Basingstoke was archdeacon of Leicester.[2] Paris knew him well, and doubtless he is the person meant. He was a friend of Simon de Montfort, and died in 1252. Paris, on the occasion of his death, speaks of him as of a very learned man.[3] He had been to Greece, and had learnt Greek, had learnt it from a Greek girl, of whose wonderful accomplishments he had strange things to tell. She could foresee eclipses, pestilences, and even earthquakes, and had taught the archdeacon all that he knew. Perhaps, while seated at her feet, he not only learnt but forgot; perhaps, as a traveller, he acquired a habit of telling good stories. At any rate the story that he told to Paris was this: 'An English deacon loved a Jewess with unlawful love, and ardently desired her embraces. "I will do what you

---

[1] *Historia Anglorum*, ii, 254.
[2] See *Dict. Nat. Biog.* s.v. Basing.
[3] *Chron. Maj.* vol. v. p. 284.

ask," said she, "if you will turn apostate, be circumcised, and hold fast the Jewish faith." When he had done what she bade him, he gained her unlawful love. But this could not long be concealed, and was reported to Stephen of Canterbury. Before him the deacon was accused; the evidence was consistent and weighty; he was convicted, and then confessed all these matters, and that he had taken open part in a sacrifice which the Jews made of a crucified boy. And when it was seen that the deacon was circumcised, and that no argument would bring him to his senses, he solemnly apostatised before the archbishop and the assembled prelates in this manner:—a cross with the Crucified was brought before him, and he defiled the cross,[1] saying, "I renounce the new-fangled law and the comments of Jesus the false prophet," and he reviled and slandered Mary the mother of Jesus, and made against her a charge not to be repeated. Thereupon the archbishop, weeping bitterly at hearing such blasphemies, deprived him of his orders. And when he had been cast out of the church, Fawkes, who was ever swift to shed blood, at once carried him off and swore, "By the throat of God! I will cut the throat that uttered such words," and dragged him away to a secret spot and cut off his head. The poor wretch was born at Coventry. But the Jewess managed to escape, which grieved Fawkes, who said, "I am sorry that this fellow goes to hell alone."'

Eye-witness and archdeacon though Master John of Basingstoke may have been, we cannot believe all that he said. In the first place, he will have the deacon's head cut off, while all our best witnesses agree about the burning. In the second place, either the charge of crucifying a boy is just the mere 'common form' charge against the Jews (the Jews were always crucifying boys,

[1] Et minxit super crucem.

as everyone knew, and were now and again slaughtered for it), or else the archdeacon has muddled up the history of the deacon with that of the labourer who was immured for crucifying himself. Nor does it seem likely that the assembled prelates gave the apostate an opportunity of manifesting his change of faith in a fashion at once very solemn and very gross. But what is said of Fawkes of Bréauté deserves consideration. Fawkes, when this story was told, was long since banished and dead, and it may well be that he had become a bugbear, a mythical monster to whom, under Satan, mischief of all sorts might properly be ascribed. But what mischief, what evil doing had there been? Why should a lawful execution be converted into a hurried and secret act of this cursing and bloodthirsty enemy of mankind, this Fawkes of Bréauté, 'ever swift to shed blood,' with imprecations about the throat of God? Certainly the impression left on the archdeacon's mind seems to have been that of a deed which was indecently hasty.

What Paris says in his *Chronica Maiora*[1] is briefer, but it has a new marvel for us, and shows that we are already on treacherous ground. He introduces us to an hermaphrodite. A man has been apprehended who has in his hands, feet, and side the five wounds of the crucifixion; he and an accomplice, a person *utriusque sexus, scilicet, Ermofroditus*, confess their offences, and are punished by the judgment of the church. 'Likewise also a certain apostate, who, being Christian, had turned Jew, a deacon, he too was judicially punished (*iudicialiter punitus*); and Fawkes at once snatched him away and caused him to be hanged (*quem Falco statim arreptum suspendi fecit*).' The poor deacon, who has been already burnt and beheaded, is now hanged. This we may pass by, nor will we discuss the question how the old woman

[1] Vol. III. p. 71.

who called herself St. Mary became an hermaphrodite; but we again notice that the slaying of the apostate is due to Fawkes, and seems a lawless or at least irregular act. Doubtless the abbey in which Paris wrote was just the place in which stories discreditable to Fawkes would be readily believed and invented, and Paris himself seems to have cherished a bitter hatred for 'the great enemy and despoiler of St. Alban's.'[1] But again we have to ask whether and why there was anything reprehensible in putting to death this degraded clerk, and, if not, why that evil principle, Fawkes of Bréauté, should be invoked to account for what was perfectly natural and right?

Another ornate version is given by Thomas Wykes, who, it is believed, wrote near the end of the thirteenth century and in the monastery of Oseney, the scene of the council.[2] 'In this council there was presented a deacon who, some time ago, had for the love of a Jewess rejected Christianity, apostatised, and been circumcised according to the Jewish rite. Being convicted of this, he was first degraded, then condemned by a secular judgment (*saeculari iudicio condemnatus*) and burnt by fire. It was said that this same apostate, in contempt of the Redeemer and of the catholic faith, had even dared to throw away in an ignoble place (*in loco ignobili*) the Lord's body which had been stolen from a church. A Jew revealed this, and in corroboration of the Christian faith the Lord's body was found unpolluted, uncorrupted, in a fair vessel, prepared for it, as one may well believe, by angel hands. And there was brought into the same council a country fellow (*rusticus*) who had come to such a pitch of madness that, to the despite of the Crucified, he had crucified himself, asserting that he was the Son of God and the Redeemer of

---

[1] Dr. Luard's Preface to vol. iii. p. xii.
[2] *Ann. Monast.* vol. iv. p. 62. See Dr. Luard's Preface, pp. x–xv.

the world. He was immured by the judgment of the Council, and shut up in prison he ended his life, fed on water and hard bread.' This is, I think, the first and only account which states that the deacon was condemned by a lay court, and I believe that it comes from too late a time to be trusted; the legend about the consecrated wafer shows that the story was already being improved by transmission.

There is not much more to be said. Later writers repeat with more or less accuracy what we have already read. Just one new ornament is added, and a pretty ornament too. Having learnt how the *rusticus* crucified himself, and how the deacon assisted at the crucifixion of a Christian boy, we may read in the pages of Holinshed and elsewhere how the council crucified an hermaphrodite: a version of the tale which good Protestants must think very proper and probable.[1]

Such being the evidence, were I to venture a guess as to what really happened, it would be this :—No one in England doubted that this deacon ought to be burnt, except, it may be, the deacon himself and his fellow Jews. It is not necessary here to assume that had his offence been mere heresy, his fate would have been the same, though I believe that of this there can be little doubt. But his crime was enormous, he had piled sin on sin. A deacon of the Christian church he had turned Jew, turned Jew for love and for the love of a Jewess. Excommunication would have awaited the king, interdict the nation, if heresy had gone unpunished, and England had lately had some sad experience of interdicts. But in such a case as this, no

---

[1] Holinshed (ed. 1807), vol. ii. p. 251. But the confusion is older; see *Polychronicon*, viii. 200; Knighton Twysden's *Scriptores*, p. 2422; it must, I think, have originated in the clerical blunder of someone who wrote *crucifixus* instead of *immuratus*.

ecclesiastical threat would be needed; everyone would agree that this self-made Jew must be burnt. It was the duty of the council to degrade him, to demand that he should be punished, to see that he was punished; but the council could not pronounce upon him any sentence beyond that of degradation. He was degraded then, not inside the church like the manslayer and the thief, but outside the church, before the people, and he was then handed over to the sheriff or his bailiffs. He was at once burnt; most of our witnesses bring out this fact that he was burnt at once, and without any further formality. Possibly it was intended that there should be some further formality, some sentence pronounced by a lay tribunal; one of our witnesses, the canon of Barnwell, seems to say as much, and the story about the indecorous haste of Fawkes points the same way. Possibly, then, Fawkes or his subordinates acted with unexpected promptitude; Fawkes, unless he is maligned, was not given to waiting for orders. One writer at the end of the century says that the man was condemned by the lay court. I take this to prove that by that time it was thought that there ought to be, assumed that there must have been, some precept from a lay tribunal, or some writ from the king. But whatever was expected and omitted was a bare formality, the registration of a foregone conclusion. By an informality the deacon gained a speedier release from a painful world. Any notion that he would have been saved, had he been brought before the king's justices, we may dismiss as idle. Those justices, almost to a man, would have been ecclesiastics, and among laymen he would have fared no better. There was no statute, there may perhaps have been no English precedent to the point; such a case is not foreseen in advance, and when it happens it is unprecedented; but that a deacon who turns **Jew** for **the love of a** Jewess **should** be burnt, needed **no** proof **whatever.** Bracton, **as I** think, knew that there had been no judgment of any lay court ('qui cum esset per episcopum degradatus, *statim* fuit igni traditus per manum laicalem'), and he fully approved of what had been done, and so far generalised the case as to state for law that **an** apostate **clerk (a** layman would have **been in** no better plight, but Bracton, as it happens, is discussing clerical privileges) is to be delivered to the lay power and burnt.

The fate **of the** man and woman who were immured, enthusiasts, **fanatics,** lunatics, impostors, or whatever they were, **is as** remarkable **as the fate of the deacon.** The notion **that for breach of monastic vows** persons were sometimes **bricked** up **in walls was once current, and** may **still be** entertained **by some who take their** *Marmion* **too seriously. Scott indeed sanctioned it** not only by **verse, but by a solemn prose note. Very** possibly **the main foundation of this notion is some** version **of the story that has here been before us, for I** believe **that this is almost all that is to be found about** immuration **in any English records or chronicles. We** see plainly (and **this might, I take it, be fully proved from** foreign books) **that our witnesses do not mean that two persons were suffocated in brick or stone. They were** imprisoned **for life, and fed on bread and water. Doubtless the imprisonment was very close and strait, otherwise we should not have the same** *immuratus* **from writer after writer when** *incarceratus* **and** *imprisonatus* **lay ready to hand, and one writer says that they were enclosed between two walls, not between four; but still they were fed, though water and hard bread were their fare. Stephen Langton was copying but too closely the proceedings of foreign inquisitors, who well knew how to 'immure' those whom they did not burn.**

Here our story ends; but, as is well known, the deacon's case became a precedent. In particular, it became a precedent for the incineration of Arians and Anabaptists when in the days of Edward VI. and Elizabeth there were no English statutes which commanded or authorised the infliction of that punishment. I am not sure that those who have discussed the fate of these unfortunates have always placed themselves at the right point of view. Heresy is a spiritual crime, and therefore it is for the church and not for the state to decide how heretics shall be punished. The church has decided that obstinate heretics shall be burnt. Whatever may have been the case in 1222, there can be no doubt what was the law of the church a few years later, and before the end of the century the Sext had made the matter quite clear. Frederick II., 'while still remaining in devotion to the Roman church,' gave the popes an opportunity of decreeing the death of heretics, and at the same time of avoiding all ugly phrases. Under what law, then, were the English Lollards burnt? Lyndwood's answer is: Under *Ut inquisitionis negotium*, c. 18 in Sexto, 5. 2. True, you will not find, nor should you expect to find there any coarse talk of flame and faggot, but you will find there quite enough: the pope wills that Frederick's constitutions be enforced throughout the world.[1]

Then we observe what happened in 1401. Parliament was in the act of making a statute which would direct the sheriff to burn the convicted heretic. William Sautre, however, was done to death before the statute was passed. The question has been raised why Archbishop Arundel was in this indecent hurry to burn his man. Readers of Lyndwood will hardly doubt what the reply should be. Arundel had obtained from the

[1] Lyndwood, p. 293, gl. ad v. *poenas in iure expressas*.

king and the lords an admission that, statute or no statute, heretics are to be burnt. They are to be burnt, for divine law and the positive law of the church require it. The aid of a statute was extremely desirable. Unless parliament helped them, the bishops would often be unable to procure the arrest and detention of suspects, and there would be frequent friction between spiritual and temporal power. It was equally desirable, however, that at least one Lollard should be burnt, not under any act of parliament, but under *Ut inquisitionis* (c. 18 in Sexto, 5. 2), in order that the right of the church to declare that obstinate heresy is a capital crime might be plainly manifested to all men as a right which no statute gave, and no parliament could take away.

When at the beginning of Edward VI.'s reign the statutes that had been passed against the Lollards, 'and all and every other act or acts of parliament concerning doctrine or matters of religion'[1] were being repealed, did those who projected this change intend that there should be no more burning? Their subsequent conduct would make us hope that this had not been their meaning; that conduct is a *contemporanea expositio*. But also we may suppose them looking at two obvious books to discover what will be the law when all statutes have been repealed. They look at Fitzherbert's *Natura Brevium*. They see there the writ under which Sautre was burnt; it is a writ which has no statute behind it; it is a writ which goes the length of saying that divine as well as human and canonical law sends the obstinate heretic to his painful death.[2] They look at Lyndwood's

[1] Stat. 1 Edw. VI. c. 12. sec. 3.
[2] *Natura Brevium*, 269; *Rolls of Parliament*, iii. 459: 'haereticos in forma praedicta convictos et damnatos iuxta legem divinam et humanam canonica instituta et in hac parte consuetudinaria ignis incendio comburi debere.'

Provinciale. So much of the old canon law is still in force as is not repugnant to the laws of God and the statutes of our lord the king. We have good reason to fear that in their eyes a law for the burning of Arians and Anabaptists was in full harmony with the word of God, and no one could say that it was condemned by any English statute. They repealed the Lancastrian edicts. Thereby they made it practically impossible for the bishops to administer the law against heresy, for, as already said, without statutory power of arrest and detention, the bishops could do very little. The prelates of the time were not to be trusted; they were Henricians; they might burn the wrong people. On the other hand, the legates *a latere* of the poor little pope-king would wield powers of arrest and detention such as the royal council wielded, and no man in those days was prepared to question its deeds. As to the authors of the *Reformatio Legum*, I know that a charitable doubt has been raised, and would gladly entertain it;[1] but where others may see uncertainty, I can see only the traditional hypocrisy of the medieval church, which leaves the nasty word unsaid but thoroughly understood. We sometimes find continuity where we would rather have found a new departure. Not only Arians and Anabaptists, but intractable Romanists and intractable Lutherans would have been burnable under the reformed law of the reformed church of England. Would the intractable Romanists have been consoled by the thought that after all they were suffering under *Ut inquisitionis* (c. 18 in Sexto, 5. 2)?

At the beginning of Elizabeth's reign it must have been notorious to all that a few heretics had been put to death in the days of her godly brother. Once more parliament was dealing with the matter. Once more

[1] Hallam, *Const. Hist.*, ed. 1832, vol. i. p. 139.

it repealed the Lancastrian statutes which Mary had revived. Once more it abstained from saying that there was to be no more burning; and a little more burning there was. The old law-books were being put into print. Everyone could read how Arundel burnt Sautre, and how Langton burnt a deacon who turned Jew for love, and the love of a Jewess.[1]

[1] For two different views of the manner in which obstinate heresy became a capital crime, see Tanon, *Histoire des tribunaux de l'inquisition*, Paris, 1893, and Julien Havet, *Œuvres*, Paris, 1896, vol. ii. p. 117 ff.

INDEX

ACADEMIC study of canon law, **92**, 97.
Acceptance of laws, 31.
Acts of Parliament, power of, **12**.
Advowsons, 62, 74, 148-157.
Albigensians, 161.
Alexander III., 62, 122-124, **145**.
Anabaptists, 176-179.
Ancharano, Petrus de, 5.
Andreae, Johannes, 7, 39, **108**.
Anti-ecclesiastical legislation, 57.
Apparitors, 34.
Appeals to Rome, **103**, 113.
Appel comme d'abus, **86**.
Apostasy, 158, 173.
Arians, 176-179.
Arrangement of *Provinciale*, 37.
Arundel, Thomas, 17, 18, 176.
Athona, Johannes de. *See* Ayton.
Authority and obedience, 2, 10.
Ayton, John of, **6, 55, 76, 98**.

BALDWIN, Archbishop, **128**.
Banns of marriage, 39.
Basel, Council of, 15.
Basingstoke, John of, **169**.
Bastardy and ordination, **55**.
  „ special, 53.
Baysio, Guido de, 8, **13**.
Beaufort, Cardinal, 15.
Becket, Thomas, 60, 62, **132-147**.
Bethmann-Hollweg, **110**.
Bishops and metropolitan, **117-120**.
  „ the universal, 116.
Bishoprics and temporalities, 151.
Bishoprics, collation to, (*c*).
Bis in idipsum, 138.
Blood, judgment of, 159-179.
Boniface VIII., 14, 28, 77, 80.
  „ of Savoy, 29, 36, 61, 64, 74.
Bosham, Herbert of, 140, 147.
Bourges, primacy of, 121.
Bracton, Henry, 60, 106, 107, 147, 163, 175.
Bréauté, Fawkes of, 163-175.
Breviarium Alarici, 142.
Burgh, John de, 40, 55, 98.

Buttrio, Antonius de, 5.
Byzantinism, 94.

CAESARO-PAPALISM, 94.
Caius College, MSS. at, 109, 121.
Cambridge, 94, 96, 97.
Canonists and divines, 116.
Canterbury, church of, 118.
Cantilupe, Thomas, 117.
Cardinals, 7.
Case-law, 44.
Cathari, 161.
Cautelae, 110.
Cawdry's case, **81**.
Chappuis, Jean, 10.
Chichele, Henry, 15, 34, 48, **69**.
Church of England, 114.
  „ the, as political **organism**, 100.
Circumspecte agatis, 79.
Civilians, English, 94-97.
Civil law, 46, 93.
Clarendon, Constitutions of, **133**.
Clement IV., 66.
  „ V., 157.
Clementines, 9, 14, **131**.
Clergy and laity, 68, 73.
  „ benefit of, 59-62, 87, 132-147.
Clerical justices, 74.
Cloister, 29, 31.
Coggeshall, Ralph of, 166.
Coke, Sir E., 156.
Commendation of benefices, 23.
Commentators, 11.
Commission, Ecclesiastical Courts, 2, 26, 46, 120, 158.
Common law, 4.
  „ lawyers, 75, 93.
  „ Pleas, Court of, 146-157.
Compilatio prima, 5.
Consent and legislation, 24, 81.
Constance, Council of, 15, 16, 71.
Constantine, donation of, 98.
Constitutions, provincial, 19.
Corpus decretorum, 47.
Corpus iuris, 10.
Councils, general, 14.

Councils, provincial, 32.
Coventry, Walter of, 167.
Cowell's *Interpreter*, 96.
Crucifixion of children, 170.
Cugnières, Pierre de, 60, 86.
Cullen, Cardinal, 58.
Curiae tradere, 141.
Custom, 10, 41.

DECRETALES Gregorii, 3, 11, 60, 131.
Decretals, how made, 18.
Decretum Gratiani, 3, 18, 61, 98, 129.
Degradation, 135, 164.
Delegates, papal, 105, 111.
Delegation of causes, 104, 119.
De multa, 149-156.
Deposition of princes, 162.
Desuetude of laws, 31.
Diceto, Ralph de, 137.
Diocesan and provincial law, 36.
Doderidge, Justice, 96.
Drawda Hall, 107.
Drogheda, William of, 107-116.
Dunstable, annals of, 165.

ECCLESIASTICAL law, the king's, 81.
  „   patronage, 62-73, 146-157.
Edward I., 30, 36.
  „   III., 150-156.
  „   VI., 177.
Elizabeth, Queen, 178.
Ely, Eustace, Bishop of, 124, 126.
Excommunication, 40.
Execrabilis, 21, 22, 148-157.
Executive and authoritative commands, 26.
  „   and legislative, 129.
Executor, testamentary, 33.
Exempt religious, 24, 103.
'Extravagantes,' 9.

FABIAN, Pope, 142.
Federal courts, 103.
Federalism in the Church, 101-105.
Felonious clerks, 60.
Feudorum Libri, 42.
Fitzherbert's *Natura Brevium*, 177.
Foliot, Gilbert, 137.
Ford, Abbot of, 128.
Forfeiture for heresy, 80.
  „   of patronage, 68.
Forum internum, 35.
France, ecclesiastical law in, 57, 60, 85.
Frederick I., 123.
  „   II., 80.

Friedberg, Dr. E., 122.
Frideswide, Cartulary of St., 107.
Fuller, Thomas, 97.

GALLICAN liberties, 85, 90.
Gardiner, Stephen, 94.
Gascoigne's *Liber Veritatum*, 72.
Gaunt, John of, 152.
Gemeines Recht, 4.
Geminiano, Dominicus de Sancto, 5, 16.
Geographical limits of competence, 113.
Gentili, Alberico, 95.
Gibson's *Codex*, 81, 97.
Gratian, 3, 129, 140.
Gregory IX., 19, 23, 37, 60, 121-123, 130.
Grosseteste, Robert, 53, 54, 59, 60, 64, 66, 116.

HALE, Sir M., 84.
Hallam, Henry, 178.
  „   Robert, 15.
Henry II., 60, 62, 132-147.
  „   III., 62.
  „   IV., 80.
  „   VIII., 82, 87, 92.
Heresy, 17, 79, 158-179.
Hildebrandine age, 101.
Hinschius, Dr. P., 17, 30, 59, 82.
Holland, Prof. T. E., 95.
Homicide, 38.
Honorius III., 130.
Hook, Dr. W. F., 146.
Horsey, Dr., 89.
Hostiensis, 115.
Hun, murder of, 89.

IGNORANCE of law, 35.
Immunity, clerical, 59, 87, 132.
Immuration, 166, 168, 175.
Imperialism, 94.
Imola, Johannes ab, 5.
Impetration, 111, 114.
Innocent III., 25, 39, 124, 130, 144, 160.
  „   IV., 66, 80.
Institutions and classes, 74.
Interpretation of statutes, 25, 33.
Ipso iure vacation, 150, 156.
Italians in England, 64.

JEWS, treatment of the, 160, 161.
John XXII., 21, 22, 149-156.
Judges, how selected, 114.
Judicial organisation, 103.
Jus commune, 4.

Jus divinum, 11, 88.
Jus naturale, 12.
Jus positivum, 88.
Justinian's books, 93, 101.

KIDDERMINSTER, Richard, 89.

LANGTON, Stephen, 78, 158.
Lapse of presentations, 77.
Lateran Council II., 107.
" III., 77.
" IV., 20, **149**, **161**, 162.
" V., 88.
Law and judgment, 129.
Lay hand, 163.
Legates *a latere*, 25.
Legatine constitutions, 25, 46.
Legatus natus, 45, 119.
Legists and decretists, 93.
Legitimation of bastards, 53.
Libelli, 111.
Liberties, ecclesiastical, 101.
Lollardy, 15, 45, 176.
Lyndwood, 4-6, 65, 78, **81, 97, 176,** 177.
Lynn, Deanery of, **150**.
Lyons, Council of, **21**, 28.

MARRIAGE, 38, 91.
Mary, Queen, 179.
Merton, Parliament of, 53.
Metropolitan power, 36, **117-120**.
Moine, Jean le, 7, 86.
Monachus, Johannes, 7, **16**.
Monarchy, ecclesiastical, 129.
Monte Lauduno, Willelmus de, 13.
Montpellier, William of, **108**.
Morins, Richard, 165.
Murimuth, Adam of, **71**.

NEPOTISM, papal, 67.
Newton, John, 8.
Nolumus leges mutare, 54.
Nuns in cloister, **27, 31**.

OBITER *dicta*, 130.
Officials, 43, 74, 119.
O'Keeffe trial, 30, 58.
Omnicompetence, 48.
Ordeal, 162.
Ordinary, the universal, 104.
Original writ, 112.
Oseney, 159.
Otto, the legate, 25, 32.
Ottobon, the legate, 20, 31.
Oxford, 94, 97, 107-111, 115.
" Councils at, 159, 161.

PAPAL *dominium*, 66, 72.
Paris, Matthew, 115, 169, 171.
Parliament and Church, 91.
Parning, Sir R., 151.
Patronage, ecclesiastical, 22, 63-73, 148-157.
Pavia, Bernard of, 37.
Pecock, Reginald, 98.
Peckham, John, 20-30, **34, 61, 65,** 115, 117-120.
Pelagius, 161.
Perplexity of causes, **119**.
Petition of 1344, 67, 70.
" 1351, 155.
Petitory action for advowsons, **71**.
Pius I., 142.
Pope and Council, 14, 16.
" power of, 11, 104.
Plenitudo potestatis, 49.
Pluralism, 20, 23, 149-157.
Praemunire, 70.
'Pragmatique' of St. **Louis, 86**.
Prelate and Council, **32**.
Prescription, 41, 65.
Primacies, 121.
Princeps, 16, 101, **128**.
Privilegium fori, **57, 132-147**.
Procurations, **10**.
Prohibition, writs of, 63, 74, 84, 111.
Provisors, 63-73, 148.
Prynne, William, 95.
Pseudo-Isidore, 101, 142.
Publication of decrees, 17, 131.
Pupilla oculi, 40.

QUARE *impedit*, 67, 150.
Questions asked of Pope, 124.
Quod permittat, 152.
Quod principi placuit, 16.

RABELAIS, 148.
Real and personal, 59.
Reasonableness of customs, 41.
Reception of laws, 82.
Redwaldus, 111.
Re-enactment of laws, 35.
Reformatio Legum, 178.
Reformation, effects of the, 56, 90.
Repair of churches, 42.
Reservation of benefices, 22, 149, 155.
Reserved cases, 102.
Reynolds, Walter, 153.
Richard II., 63.
" Archbishop of Canterbury, 126.
Ritual, 41.
Roffredus, 121.

Roman court, 45.
" practice, 45.
Roaldus, 111.
Rosarium, 8, 13.
Rota, 44, 62.
Rural deans, 43.

SALISBURY, use of, 41.
Salmon, John, 150.
Sandale, John, 152.
Sandy and Potton, 123.
Sautre, William, 158.
Schulte, J. F. von, 39, 108.
Scott, Sir Walter, 175.
Selden, John, 97.
Separation of powers, 129.
Sext, 10, 28, 31, 35, 131, 176.
Si non omnes, 112.
Si quis suadente, 102.
Socinus, Marianus, 7.
Somerset, Protector, 94.
Spiritual and temporal, 56.
Standish, Henry, 87.
State, definition of a, 100.
Stephen, Pope, 142.
Stillingfleet's *Ecclesiastical Cases*, 84.
Stratford, John, 6, 23, 34.
Stratton Audley, 109.
Stubbs, Dr. W., 6, 52.
Summa Aurea, 109.
Supremacy, royal, 147.

TANCRED, 104.
Tenths, papal, 13.

Testamentary causes, 42, 59.
Threats, papal, 127.
Tithes, 42, 84, 125.
Toledo, primacy of, 121.
Town and gown, 111.
Trial of clerks, 136.

ULTRA vires statuentis, 20.
Unam sanctam, 14, 30, 94.
Universitas causarum, 119.
Universities, 90, 98.
Usurpations, papal and archiepiscopal, 117, 120.
Ut inquisitionis, 176.

VAS electionis, 7, 10.
Vicar of God, 147.
Vincennes, dispute at, 60, 86.
Visitation fees, 10.

WIMBLEDON, church of, 152.
Winchcombe, Abbot of, 87, 89.
Winchelsea, Robert, 152, 153.
Wolsey, Cardinal, 80.
Writs, papal, 107.
Wyche, Richard, 46.
Wycliffe, 15.
Wykes, Thomas, 172.

YEAR-BOOKS, 44, 151–153.
York, Books at, 8.

ZABARELLIS, Franciscus de, 7.
Zenzelinus, 8.

www.ingramcontent.com/pod-product-compliance
Lightning Source LLC
Chambersburg PA
CBHW020240170426
43202CB00008B/168